EQUIPPED
TO LEAD

EQUIPPED TO LEAD

MANAGING PEOPLE, PROCESS, PARTNERS, AND PERFORMANCE

DAN J. SANDERS
GALEN WALTERS

New York   Chicago   San Francisco   Lisbon   London   Madrid
Mexico City   Milan   New Delhi   San Juan   Seoul
Singapore   Sydney   Toronto

The McGraw·Hill Companies

1 2 3 4 5 6 7 8 9 0   DOC/DOC   0 9 8

MHID   0-07-159100-1
ISBN 978-0-07-159100-3

This publication is designed to provide accurate and authoritative information in regard to the subject matter covered. It is sold with the understanding that neither the author nor the publisher is engaged in rendering legal, accounting, or other professional service. If legal advice or other expert assistance is required, the services of a competent professional person should be sought.

> —*From a Declaration of Principles jointly adopted*
> *by a Committee of the American Bar*
> *Association and a Committee of Publishers*

McGraw-Hill books are available at special quantity discounts to use as premiums and sales promotions, or for use in corporate training programs. To contact a representative please visit the Contact Us pages at www.mhprofessional.com.

This book is printed on acid-free paper.

For my aunt, Liz Smith,
whose life represents the incarnation of the ideals
we should all pursue.

—DAN J. SANDERS

✦

To Mikki, my beautiful wife and closest friend.

—GALEN WALTERS

CONTENTS

FOREWORD

Equipped to Lead is where inspiration meets innovation. That is the thought that kept coming
back to me as I read this excellent manuscript. Leaders should understand, perhaps more than anything,
how important it is to inspire innovation among their
people.

Nothing much happens in business today without
people, and people without passion cannot make great
contributions to an organization.

Passion is power, and any leader able to inspire his
or her group to work together will soon find success
is contagious. Dan Sanders and Galen Walters impart
this logical message using wonderful language and
practical examples in a way that will connect with any
leader, regardless of the organization that person is
leading.

Equipped to Lead is not a quick-fix leadership
manual. All of us pick up books from time to time,
looking for one new idea to incorporate into our day-
to-day business routines. This book offers so much
more—a leadership approach that can create the most
rewarding experience of your career. For those of you
who still believe the only ultimate end is profits: read
this book, and "if you apply it, they will come."Dan

and Galen remind us that leadership is a daily responsibility, a matter of constantly refining our routines. A modification here. A change there. It is an ongoing growth process—for the leader and the organization. If we are not moving forward, we have truly stopped. I keep coming back to the inspirational aspect of leadership. It is a significant element that is driven home so eloquently in this work. Great leaders talk the talk, then they walk the walk. Both are essential to keep an organization moving forward.

Dan and Galen give us an accurate picture of what is happening in the business world today in the Knowledge Age. Leaders need to be ready to grapple with all of the challenges that will confront them in the weeks, months, and years ahead. The points they make about all different-sized companies are worth remembering. They discuss the growing focus that is being placed on sustainability. I see this in many different businesses, and I believe it is just a small beginning of what is to come.

Those leaders who can place their organizations on the path to sustainability will set the pace for others. The best way to find that path, as Dan and Galen advocate, is to engage your people in the organization's mission and vision and turn passion loose. As I liked to remind our people: "Sometimes you have to go out on a limb because that's where the fruit is."

An overriding message of this book—work should enrich our lives and the lives of others—should resonate with each of us, regardless of the role we play in our respective work environments. *Equipped to Lead* tells us that leaders are made, not born. I believe that is true, provided people are mentored and guided in a proactive manner early and often in their careers. We have leaders all around us who may not yet know they are leaders. They are waiting, and it is the responsibility of the current leaders to bring others along, nurture them by giving them the freedom to make mistakes, and show them the way.

Another aspect of leadership evident within these pages tells us leaders are honor bound to challenge themselves and those around them. I am a CPA, and in the early history of our firm, the partners would discuss our growth and the need to expand our office facilities. Whatever number of people we projected we would have, I always leased space that was a multiple of that number. Of course, sometimes the other partners thought I was crazy, but you have to stretch yourself. That is a prescription for organizations to exceed their own expectations.

Another thread that weaves through *Equipped to Lead* is the emphasis on people and teamwork. I remember a client whose business was not progressing the way he had hoped, so he decided to sell. I was helping him negotiate with a buyer, and they finally agreed on a price. Then, the seller started asking questions. He asked about transferring the plant lease. He asked about assigning equipment contracts. He asked about taking the inventory. Each time, the buyer indicated he wasn't interested in those aspects of the business. "You keep them," he said. Finally, the seller asked "What are you doing?"

The buyer's reply was simple and telling. "I'm buying your people," he said. Right then, I think the seller realized his past mistakes.

Years ago, I designed a promotional brochure for our firm that focused on people, passion, and performance. Dan and Galen introduce the 4P Management System in this work, and their thoughts run parallel to my own in terms of providing a practical system for leaders to maximize the power and passion of their workforce.

Equipped to Lead should be required reading for leaders from all walks of life. The topics touched on here cut across the spectrum. My experience with many different-sized businesses, in leading professional associations, in interacting with government agencies, and in my work with nonprofits convinces me that these principles work in any organization.

The authors speak with a unique blend of compassion and authority. They understand how an organization's philosophy, values, and reputation in the marketplace as well as its sustainability boil down to one common denominator: people with purpose. Any organization should have a mission statement, but that vision has to be a group effort. It cannot be put to paper, locked up in the boss's office and looked over once or twice a year. Everyone in the organization has to have ownership in it. In our early vision statement, we wanted to be a "unique passionate firm making innovative contributions to our clients and our community." That is what Dan and Galen continually remind us—being *Equipped to Lead* is more than an everyday routine.

What is the real test of leadership in any organization? It is what happens to that organization after the leader departs. If the leader did his or her job properly, the operation will not only continue but will survive, thrive, and move on to higher levels of contributions to people and our communities.

In closing, I am reminded of an old Chinese proverb:

> If you want a year of prosperity, grow grain.
> If you want 10 years of prosperity, grow trees.
> If you want 100 years of prosperity, grow people.

It is my hope that as you read this book, it prepares you and your organization for long-term prosperity.

Thomas W. Rimerman, CPA
Former Chairman, American Institute
of Certified Public Accountants

PREFACE

There it sat. Buried in a stack of book proposals and unsolicited manuscripts, the query letter for *Built to Serve*, the precursor to this book, could easily have been overlooked. Editors working for global publishing companies receive thousands of such letters each week. No one would have known, much less cared, if one more unsolicited letter had found its way into the trash heap.

However, an unexpected event occurred. McGraw-Hill Professional Trade Group released *Built to Serve* in the fall of 2007, and, surprisingly, it became an overnight success, landing on the *New York Times* and *USA Today Money* bestseller lists. Why? How? *Built to Serve* was the work of a first-time author—an active chief executive who was new to the public discourse regarding leadership. Despite that, or perhaps even because of that, something resonated with readers around the globe.

Perhaps it was this bold and simple claim: *The global business culture that prevails today is broken. Leaders have spent far too much time focusing on fiscal resources and not enough time focusing on human resources. Long-term success is a result of putting more effort into building a positive, people-centered culture than into poring over profit-and-loss statements.*

Rest assured that this was not the kind of message that the business world wanted to embrace. Immediate reactions to the premise of *Built to Serve* included shock, surprise, and outright disdain. These emotion-driven counterpoints and criticisms were not unforeseen, but the fervor and tone with which they were delivered were alarming. However, despite the intense efforts of some entrenched and organized pundits eager to defend the status quo—a condition largely defined by flawed workplace cultures—the book's message prevailed.

The strength of *Built to Serve* was not its complex presentation of scholarly ideals, but its simple delivery of timeless, universal logic and truth. The mass appeal of the book initiated a workplace movement driven by culture and synergy. Organizational leaders began to realize that the bottom line *can* be driven by people-first practices. But they needed help—simple, proven tools that could be implemented easily.

Hence, this work.

In *Equipped to Lead*, you will discover no-nonsense methods and applications for execution, including a much deeper explanation of the real link between *Built to Serve* and *Equipped to Lead* called the 4P Management System—a proven approach to restoring order and balance amid organizational chaos. This system, which focuses exclusively on people, process, partners, and performance, provides the foundation for sustained success regardless of an organization's size, industry, or locale.

And it is so much more. Current subscribers to the 4P Management System have developed a greater understanding of the idea that sustainable businesses must be about more than price and profit. They must be about purpose and about people who are like-minded in their desire to make a positive impact not only on the economy, but also on humanity.

Such a dynamic was in place 15 years ago when we, the authors, first crossed paths. We were like-minded when it came to recognizing the need for a radical transformation, a paradigm shift aimed at reshaping the way people approach and comprehend the true nature of the work they do, filling so much of their time.

For nearly seven years, we worked together within the confines of what we considered to be a covenant relationship. It was more than a friendship, more than a partnership. It was a relationship that was made almost sacred by the amounts of mutual trust and respect between the two people involved.

Working within the spirit of this relationship, we sometimes made progress, and we sometimes took two steps back. Sometimes it seemed that we did both at the same time. During that period, particularly between 1997 and 2002, we experienced the extremes that are inherent in owning a business.

We shared the exhilaration of landing big accounts and successfully closing on business acquisitions, but we also became well acquainted with the frustration of trying to grow a company primarily on our own with nothing more than cash flow. Likewise, we struggled to manage properly those diverse business units employing more than a thousand people in multiple locations, separated in some cases by thousands of miles. Frankly, the complexity of our challenges, coupled with a rapidly changing business climate, often was overwhelming.

Thanks to this journey, we became absolutely convinced that leaders need the proper tools for service. They must be equipped to succeed because the stakes are high and failure is not an option. In fact, for us, what began as a study of leadership became a revelation regarding the importance of organizational excellence for the long-term viability of all civilizations. No longer could the influence of one leader be judged in the context of one organization, one industry, or even one nation—it had to be considered in much broader, global terms.

This realization prompted a great sense of urgency to challenge all leaders, including ourselves, to align our beliefs with our practices immediately. A reluctance to accept this critical concept almost certainly means never tapping into the unrealized potential within people and organizations. Perhaps British historian Arnold J. Toynbee, whose thoughts weave all of our chapters together, said it best in his essay "Civ-ilization on Trial": "Practice unsupported by belief is a wasting asset."

Equally important, if Toynbee's conclusion that no evidence afforded by history warrants any hope that human nature will ever change for the better or for the worse is accurate, then our only hope for improving civilization is found in individual spirituality imbuing a higher purpose and genuine fulfillment. It is precisely this thinking—that our spiritual beliefs create a catharsis in our human practices—that leaders around the world should embrace.

ACKNOWLEDGMENTS

Equipped to Lead is a compendium not just of ideals, but of two lifetimes of memorable first-hand experiences inside and alongside organizations. Here, today, as we reflect on our lives, we are both humbled by the magnitude of our blessings, starting with the people we have come to know.

Beyond the influence of our business relationships, we gratefully acknowledge the exceptional staff at McGraw-Hill Professional Trade Group in New York. The entire team represents competence and professionalism of the highest order. This book marks the second collaborative effort with gifted editor and dear friend Mary Glenn. And, this project, like the first, proved an extraordinary experience—largely because of Mary's constant encouragement and on-target recommendations.

Additionally, *Equipped to Lead* is the second project completed with the capable assistance of team members employed by The Center for Corporate Culture and The Dollins Group. Many thanks especially to Claude Dollins, Dan Dollins, and LeeAnne Grosnik for providing the necessary resources to complete the manuscript on time. Included in this effort are the fine work of Dollins Group team member Doug Hensley and the editorial assistance of Texas Tech University professors Robert and Marijane Wernsman. Together, they ensured that our thoughts and stories had structure and meaning. As a result, the manuscript reflects a marked improvement over our initial efforts. Thanks also to Yelu Hu for his help in shaping the 4P Assessment Code that is part of this work.

Information for Chapter 12 was gathered from a variety of sources, including company Web sites, the Great Places To Work Institute Web site, and the 2007 Great Places To Work Best Practices conferences. The authors salute all of these entities for the great attention they pay to people, processes, partners, and performance.

Dan Sanders thanks his wife, Shanna, his daughter, Shaley, and his son, Travis, for their unending love and support. Additionally, he expresses gratitude to his parents, L. J. and Virginia Sanders, and his mother-in-law, Jean Renfrow, for their continual encouragement. He also thanks Garry and Kim Baccus, Cecil and Diane Fincher, Joe and Jonell Hutchins, and Rick and Kerry Peters for lasting friendships unchanged by geographic separation or extended time apart. Finally, he wishes to acknowledge the many relatives, colleagues, and mentors who shaped and influenced his life for good.

Galen Walters wishes to thank his wife, Mikki, and his daughters, Amber and Molly, for their unselfish support. And he wishes to thank his father, Elbert, for instilling a can-do attitude into the five children in his family, and his mother, Clara, for her hard-working example of prayer and discipline. He also wishes to say "thank you" to the team of employees at adplex, some of whom readers will meet in this book, including Lewis Smith, Shirley Harris, Fred Stallings, Nazeeh Kaleh, Dan Thurman, Terry Sabom, Russell Anderson, Robert Johnson, Bob Nuelle, Ed Raine, Gary Sherburne, Karen McKee, Allen Ruch, Mike Krause, John Leonard, Josh Bruin, Robin Cole, and hundreds more. Thanks to Randy Casey for a lifetime friendship. Thanks also to Michael Starr, John Coats, and Pam Coats for their years of support. Thanks to Dr. Leonard Berry, author of *Discovering the Soul of Service* and *Management Lessons from the Mayo Clinic*, for his friendship, support, and inspiration.

Finally, we wish to thank God the Father, the Creator of all things good, including all the necessary tools to equip leaders properly. We pray that this book and all of the efforts spawned by this work will seek to glorify Him.

EQUIPPED TO LEAD

"I don't believe a committee can write a book. It can, oh, govern a country, perhaps, but I don't believe it can write a book."

—Arnold J. Toynbee (1889–1975)

INTRODUCTION

In today's global business culture, organizations suffer from a common yet deadly malady. Hidden behind the hype of creative advertising campaigns and masked by a steady flow of financial reporting and a seemingly endless barrage of meetings, a serious shortage of competent leaders threatens every organization's future success.

Leaders need to be *Equipped to Lead* for service. Leadership expert Dr. John W. Gardner had it right: despite what seem like a great many depressing aspects of management, leadership development is not one of them. The skills necessary for effective leadership are learned. In short, leaders are made, not born.

At the heart of the matter rests a universal truth that every stakeholder should embrace: long-term success is impossible unless leaders have a proven method for ensuring order and balance in organizational management. This truth disturbs us because most organizations these days reflect chaos and instability more than order and balance—a telltale sign of floundering leadership.

Too often, today's stakeholders rely on ill-equipped leaders to face the challenges of a postcapitalist era. In his book *Post-Capitalist Society*, the late über-management guru Peter Drucker made a compelling argument that knowledge, not capital, is the new measure of wealth. Drucker suggested that the future of business will belong to the best-led and best-managed organizations, not the biggest, oldest, or best-funded.

Given the frequent demise of big, old, and well-funded organizations, it is only appropriate that stakeholders should heed Drucker's advice and devote more time to grooming people to lead than seeking investors to woo for capital.

Regrettably, turnover among leaders is at an all-time high. According to a survey conducted by the outplacement firm Challenger, Gray & Christmas, nearly eight chief executive officers (CEOs) exited each business day in 2006. And why not? Instead of equipping leaders for success, stakeholders resort to managing leaders these days in the same way that teenagers manipulated pinball machines before electronic games became the rage.

As a result, leaders ricochet from one quarter to the next, spurred on by analysts and investors pushing buttons for faster growth and immediate returns. Amid this chaos and instability, it seems that stakeholders care more about *how* an organization is doing than about *what* an organization is doing.

Like it or not, the global business culture has come to concern itself with performance above all else. In part, this thinking is perpetuated because numbers represent a *tangible* common language, one that is easily translated, unlike the *intangible* nature of human relations. Once we factor human beings into the equation, business math becomes exceedingly difficult.

Different languages, lifestyles, and cultural influences are major obstacles to management. Leaders of organizations bog down in digesting such complexity, and they routinely opt to embrace the universal simplicity of numbers. Sadly, stakeholders fail to grasp this simple reality: it is people with knowledge who drive the bottom line, and therefore leaders must commit to people-first practices if they desire sustainable superior performance.

In addition to the ease of translating numbers, performance appeals to stakeholders because implicit in every bottom line is some measure of accountability for the leader. Unfortunately, stakeholders seem content with allowing the profit-and-loss (P&L) statement to serve as the sole indicator of a leader's performance.

Lost in the math is the inability of any P&L statement to reveal an organization's unrealized potential —a much more interesting and telling bit of information. Only leaders know to what extent their organizations failed to perform up to their potential. And as long as leaders feel compelled to pore over financial reports to the exclusion of the human resources responsible for productivity and innovation, they, too, may be ill equipped to answer this important question.

Such is the case today in many organizations. Leaders and their stakeholders need to be reminded of the importance of human beings and the processes that they employ in the Knowledge Age. This is a distressing commentary on the modern global business culture, and yet it is entirely accurate. Human beings and processes, not performance, must dominate the future dialogue between stakeholders and organizational leaders. This is a new day.

Drucker expressed it this way:

> International economic theory is obsolete. The traditional factors of production—land, labor, and capital—are becoming restraints rather than driving forces. Knowledge is becoming the one critical production factor. It has two incarnations: Knowledge applied to existing processes, services, and products is productivity; knowledge applied to the new is innovation.

Like so many Druckerisms, the power of this statement is outshone only by the accuracy of its claim. In this case, the truth is self-evident: human beings and the processes they use matter to organizations more today than at any other time in history. If organizations seek productivity in order to improve their performance, they must first seek talent and efficient processes. If organizations seek innovation in order to compete favorably, they first must mine the rich vein of knowledge possessed by the talent they employ.

An understanding of these fundamental concepts establishes a fertile field in which the seeds of order and balance can take root, despite the winds of change. What is required today is the production of a radically different crop in which old management practices lie fallow while new ideas and concepts thrive with cultivation.

Even the most forward-thinking organizations may be struggling with this profound shift in modern management. Their leaders may fear words like *order* and *balance* because they sound constrictive, capable of choking the life out of creativity and innovation. In truth, creativity and innovation thrive when talented people receive direction and context for their work.

Since the beginning of recorded history, the world's most creative and innovative human beings have discovered and rediscovered the power of order and balance. In her compelling book *Leadership and the New World—Discovering Order in a Chaotic World*, author Margaret J. Wheatley suggests that the discoveries and theories of new science, particularly during the past century, prove the inherent orderliness of the universe, with creative processes and dynamic, continuous changes that still maintain order. Based on these findings, Wheatley wrote:

I no longer believe that organizations are inherently unmanageable in this world of constant flux and unpredictability. Rather, I believe that our present ways of organizing are outmoded, and that the longer we remain entrenched in our old ways, the further we move from those wonderful breakthroughs in understanding that the world of science calls "elegant." The layers of complexity, the sense of things being beyond our control and out of control, are but signals of our failure to understand a deeper reality of organizational life, and of life in general.

What is lacking among today's leaders is not so much intellect as useful instruction—practical tools for effecting change. As in flying an airplane at supersonic speed, mastery is found not in intellectually understanding the purpose of all the gauges and switches (this is a given), but in knowing which gauges and switches to focus on during crucial stages of flight.

The same can be said for leadership in today's global business culture. Mastery is found not in intellectually understanding the importance of performance (this is a given), but in knowing how to focus on key areas of the organization at precisely the right time to maximize productivity and innovation.

We intend *Equipped to Lead* to serve as a natural segue from the intellectual understanding outlined in *Built to Serve* to a practical system of execution. Without execution, even the most brilliant intellectual concepts become nothing more than academic opinion, appropriate for the classroom but of little value inside organizations, where application is all that matters.

Fortunately, a methodology exists for providing leaders with the training they need if they are to establish order and balance amid organizational turmoil. The methodology begins with a rebirth of values and correct principles. Dr. Gardner was fond of saying, "Values always decay over time. Societies that keep their values alive do so not by escaping the process of decay but by powerful processes of regeneration."

Leaders can and should spearhead renewal when it comes to values, but they also need simple solutions to improve operational execution. Like regeneration, operational execution is also nothing more than a series of processes. *Equipped to Lead* explores this idea in great detail, but before a leader can focus on the finer points of "blocking and tackling," consideration must be given to establishing a strong foundation—a basis upon which the blocking and tackling can succeed.

Truth must be central to any meaningful solution. Dr. Stephen R. Covey captured the attention of millions nearly two decades ago with his compelling teachings on the subject of timeless, universal truths. In his bestselling book *Principle-Centered Leadership*, Dr. Covey wrote:

Correct principles are like compasses: they are always pointing the way. And if we know how to read them, we won't get lost, confused, or fooled by conflicting voices and values. Principles are self-evident, self-validating natural laws. They don't change or shift. They provide "true north" direction to our lives when navigating the "streams" of our environments.

Indeed, inherent in the concept of principle-based leadership is the understanding that *stability* stems from respecting and living by God's natural laws, which cannot be circumvented. For example, the natural law of harvest dictates that one reaps what one sows. Dr. Covey's writings on the subject beautifully illustrate, among other things, the need for faith in our lives, which, in turn, helps to bring order and balance to organizations. Intellectually, leaders must understand the moral obligation they have to their followers—they must acknowledge the innate moral compass that God provided.

But putting a key concept into practice requires much more than simply acknowledging that key concept. Initiating a purposeful movement requires hard work—a meaningful commitment to a higher purpose. Beneath the surface of any such effort, there is a strong undercurrent that attempts to pull leaders away from where they want to go. The power of societal culture is undeniable.

Nowhere is the tide of secular influence more dangerous than in the heart and head of an organization's leader. When leaders fail to live by God's natural laws and principles, organizational order and balance remains impossible. Leaders choosing to pursue this path will find an endless supply of chaos, restlessness, and instability.

Modern management requires leaders to resist the pull of societal culture and its growing willingness to exclude God and His natural laws and principles from organizations. Leaders must recognize the moral compass that is built into the soul of human beings and strive to instill the practice of ethical behavior.

Simply put, order will emerge when leaders subscribe to godly values. Without values and adherence to natural laws and principles, order cannot serve as an organization's foundation. Similarly, without adequate focus on four universal components that are common to all organizations, balance cannot take shape. These four components are the 4Ps Management System.

First, leaders must never neglect their employees— the talented *people* who represent the lifeblood of productivity and innovation within every sustainable organization.

Second, leaders must devote adequate time to the *processes* by which work flows through the organization—

the system of inputs and outputs that people use to drive productivity.

Third, leaders must acknowledge they cannot survive without *partners*—both the people who supply the organization and the people who purchase goods and services from the organization.

And, fourth, leaders must deliver superior *performance*—based on the realized potential of the organization, not the historical trend.

The 4Ps Management System begins and ends with human beings connected by processes. Performance is simply a scorecard, a historical record depicting the success of managing the first three Ps—nothing more and nothing less.

Leaders must restore and maintain order and balance in their organizations by educating stakeholders on the importance of people, processes, and partners. Only then will organizations realize revolutionary performance, soaring beyond expectations to a place of realized potential. Businessman Scott Cook, the founder of Intuit, says, "When you do something truly revolutionary, most competitors will never copy it; they won't even understand it."

Equipped to Lead will explore each of these topics in detail. Moving from the chaos of modern culture to the universal components found in every organization on the face of the earth, leaders will learn what it takes to embark on a journey of renewal—a journey that returns human beings and their passion to a rightful place of prominence in God's plan.

We believe that the journey will be worthwhile, and that the benefits of gained knowledge will allow every leader to establish and maintain order and balance amid the organizational turmoil that is prevalent today.

"Of the twenty-two civilizations that have appeared in history, nineteen of them collapsed when they reached the moral state the United States is in now."

—ARNOLD J. TOYNBEE (1889–1975)

CHAPTER 1

REAL PERVASIVE CHAOS

We live in a disruptive age—an exceedingly fast-paced world characterized by a confluence of greed and individualism. Although this may sound like a harsh indictment, today's leaders may find that maintaining order and balance amid unrestrained personal pride and the time constraints posed by social and professional obligations is becoming increasingly difficult. Time-starved people find themselves facing challenges at every turn.

Even so, most of us have adapted so successfully to the confusion of modern life that we no longer notice the destructive nature of surrendering to it. In many ways, we have capitulated to the inevitable result of a disruptive age: a chaotic culture in which success—commonly defined by power, position, and money—is inextricably linked to the pursuit of happiness.

Nowhere is this chaos more evident than in our relationships at work and at home. On-the-job relationships are changing because organizations are shifting. The notion of long-term interdependence—a secure career marked by a mutual need between employer and employee—is all but gone. What is developing today is a myopic workplace fueled by a broken system of incompetent leaders, fickle investors, and project-driven outworkers who are short on loyalty.

Ideally, organizational strategic planning should include meaningful discussions regarding the true purpose of the organization—a vision for the future, a future 10 or 20 years down the road that outlines a legacy, not just a financial forecast. Such meetings should be marked by a measure of confidence in the team's ability to overcome the unknowns because so much of the dialogue ought to revolve around potential and a high level of trust.

Nowadays, however, many organizations craft long-range plans on a foundation of uncertainty, supported by little more than a 12- to 18-month outlook. Most company meetings are marked by insecurity and a focus on cutting current costs—a telltale sign of leadership without hope.

Herb Meyer, a respected author and national intelligence expert, recognized this trend several years ago. Meyer has a good record when it comes to predicting the future—he was widely credited with being the first government official to accurately forecast the collapse of the Soviet Union. Addressing a large audience of CEOs during a speech in Seattle, Washington, Meyer made this comment regarding the major transformation taking place in the business world:

> Employers can't guarantee jobs anymore because they don't know what their companies will look like next year. Everyone is on their way to becoming an independent contractor. The new workforce contract will be, "Show up at my office five days this week and do what I want you to do, but you handle your own insurance, benefits, health care and everything else."

Arguably, the seeds of chaos actually took root almost a half-century ago during the 1960s counterculture. That movement, followed by the New Age appeal of the 1970s, the unbridled greed that drove the 1980s stock market, and the dot-com rage of the 1990s, allowed chaos to flourish.

Add to those powerful influences devastating natural disasters and deadly terrorist activity since the turn of the century, and the effect on society is that modern life is unpredictable and perhaps more narcissistic than at any other time in history. Put another way, modern life is downright messy.

Interestingly, these days, management gurus such as Tom Peters say that we should be "thriving on chaos," not rejecting it. In fairness to Peters, the context of his admonition to business leaders involves creating flexibility, fast-paced innovation, and differentiation—all of which are worthy, important ideas.

So much revolutionary talk is unnecessary. In fact, as Jim Collins pointed out in *Good to Great*, dramatic events that transform an organization rarely happen in a revolutionary manner. In speaking of organizations with sustainable transformation, Collins wrote, "There was no single defining action, no grand program, no one killer innovation, no solitary lucky break, no miracle moment."

That is bad news for consultants hyping a cure-all solution or for selfish investors bent on identifying the mother of all synergies that is certain to make them a quick buck. Lost in all of the discourse is the real purpose of life—personally and professionally.

But what may be bad news for consultants and egotistical investors is, in fact, great news for people who actually work all day, every day, to create something. Call it a higher purpose—a set of guiding principles that forms a foundation capable of withstanding disorder.

As Collins discovered after concluding his five-year study, "It is impossible to have a great life without a meaningful life. And it is very difficult to have a meaningful life without meaningful work. Perhaps, then, you might gain that rare tranquility that comes from knowing that you've had a hand in creating something of intrinsic excellence that makes a contribution."

Frankly, we are desperate for tranquility and self-sacrifice today. In short, we are desperate for an absence of chaos and a sense of fulfillment that all of us long for deep inside. It is frightening to think of a world consumed with disorder and marked by self-centeredness, but we are moving in that direction at breakneck speed—corporately and personally.

Dr. David Callahan, author of *The Cheating Culture*, suggests that a widespread shift in dominant values is driving a compelling market ideology in society and creating a culture of dishonesty, symptomatic of deep anxiety and insecurity. He wrote, "I see three changes as especially connected to the rise in cheating: individualism has morphed into a harder-edged selfishness; money has become more important to people; and harsher norms of competition have spread, while compassion for the weaker or less capable has waned."

For example, Callahan illustrates the focus on individualism that is prevalent in today's society by pointing to the recent shift in advertising by the last bastion of institutionalism: the U.S. Army. Faced with dwindling numbers of new recruits, America's military leaders opted to dispense with the well-known recruiting slogan, "Be all that you can be," featuring Army teams working together, in favor of a more appealing pitch, "An Army of one." While the spirit of the recent slogan is intended to suggest that the Army's powerful force comes from the strength of its individual soldiers, the visuals promote a somewhat entrepreneurial, cavalier approach to military service.

It is ironic that the military, which is known for a culture characterized by order and balance, would deliberately seek recruits who want to go it alone, but it is a testament to recruiting in a disruptive age—one to which even our oldest institutions struggle to adapt.

The Army is not the only organization that is influenced by factors affecting lifestyles at home. Many organizations, including nonprofits, are experiencing pervasive chaos. When people arrive at work each day, they do not abandon the demands of a busy life at home just because they are at work. They tend to carry those demands with them wherever they go. It is the cumulative effect of such high expectations that leaves people feeling as though they are falling further and further behind.

At home, family relationships are changing because families are changing. Family-friendly activities— wholesome events that once built family unity and created cherished memories—are becoming more difficult to orchestrate. Parents and children alike are subjected to a steady barrage of technology, unfiltered entertainment content, and exceedingly high self-imposed personal expectations.

According to brand futurist Martin Lindstrom, the typical 21-year-old has spent 5,000 hours playing video games, spent more than 10,000 hours on a mobile telephone, exchanged 250,000 e-mails or instant messages, and logged more than 3,000 hours on the Internet. In fact, Lindstrom points out that the Hollywood movie industry is roughly one-half the size of the burgeoning video game industry.

As a result, people are increasingly drawn to activities marked by a new, contemporary type of socialization—one that advocates self-interest above the common interest. Sadly, this modern movement leaves those without enough money to satisfy their wants feeling frustrated and those with enough money to pursue their material desires feeling empty. Either way, the modern movement toward self-gratification leaves far too many young people unfulfilled.

Not surprisingly, advertising and media experts see this predicament through a different lens—one that clearly reveals an opportunity to exploit consumers emotionally. Those experts remind us that we are entitled to whatever we desire, even if economic realities hinder our ability to pay the price.

Using the carrot-and-stick method of enticement, companies offer a variety of payment options, and credit card companies stand ready to fulfill our desires for immediate satisfaction, as long as we agree to a modern form of indentured servitude. The high cost of succumbing to a world marked by absolute individuality is not measured in dollars but in the forfeiture of a legacy larger than ourselves.

While it is true that sociologists disagree on the multitude of influences affecting the shift from "we" to "me," one factor is certain: the ubiquitous access to media content from around the world is changing the way we view our present circumstances. Dr. Benjamin Barber, author of the mesmerizing book *Consumed*, suggests that Americans have embraced a sort of "civic schizophrenia" as a result of consumer frailty. "For in the absence of real wants and genuine needs," Barber writes, "consumers often seem to invite the producer of goods and services to tell them what it is that they want."

The resulting vulnerability found in a culture of consumerism alters one's frame of reference. Consequently, people no longer compare themselves to the Joneses next door; instead, they compare themselves to the images broadcast or downloaded into their homes each day and night. In her compelling book *The Overspent American*, Boston College sociology professor Juliet Schor wrote:

> Today a person is more likely to be making comparisons with, or choose as a "reference group," people whose incomes are three, four, or five times his or her own. Advertising and the media have played an important part in stretching out reference groups vertically. When twenty-somethings can't afford much more than a utilitarian studio but think they should have a New York apartment to match the ones they see on *Friends*, they are setting unattainable consumption goals for themselves, with dissatisfaction as a predictable result. When

the children of affluent suburban and impoverished inner-city households both want the same Tommy Hilfiger logo emblazoned on their chests and the top-of-the-line Swoosh on their feet, it's a potential disaster.

The power of brands is undeniable, and their effect on human beings is just beginning to be understood. In a compelling exposé, Alissa Quart, the author of *Branded*, makes a convincing argument that the pursuit of opulence among young people is destructive. "Teens and Tweens," she wrote, "are more vulnerable and more open to a warped relationship that the brands are selling to them. It's an emptied-out relationship where they pour themselves into a brand and see themselves through objects, rather than through people or ideas."

Biblical truth teaches that we should use objects and love people; but nowadays the ironic tendency is to love objects and use people. Who is to blame for such a sad commentary? Subscribing to social Darwinism might make it easier to condone such behavior as apropos for a society known to make judgments regarding one's value based exclusively on one's outward appearance.

After all, this would be in keeping with a culture powered by materialism. But arriving at such a conclusion would represent more of a statement about the failure of leadership and personal choice, than about the incalculable value of human beings.

21

Americans in particular are vulnerable to this form of personal conflict because cupidity plays such an important role in our chaotic society, especially among younger generations. Additionally, social policy regarding the workplace is outdated and requires reform. Unlike those in other countries, where flexible scheduling and labor practices promote greater fairness among employees and their families, U.S. labor laws continue to lag.

Companies would be more capable of overcoming chaos and restoring order if their leaders had a reasonable approach to leading—one that included a balanced perspective on business and a solid grounding in faith-based principles. Such a transformation would help leaders and their teams rise to meet the challenge of another major problem contributing to pervasive chaos: unexpected events.

One of the greatest weaknesses of the human condition is its inability to understand what it does not know. We may think that we have a good handle on the daily challenges confronting us, but the fact is that we will all be convicted by our lack of knowledge eventually.

For example, as a result of the devaluation of the dollar in 1986, trouble came calling so suddenly at adplex that we really never had time to react. The dollar was devalued by more than 25 percent in a week, when previously it had never lost more than 5 percent of its value in a year.

The immediate result was a loss of 50 percent of our margin through an increase in paper costs. This was an event inflicted upon the company; it was not the result of anything our company did or did not do. Nevertheless, it placed us in a vicious tailspin, and the ground was closing in fast. A few senior leaders moved into a crisis-management mode that had never before been seen at adplex.

It was not a pleasant climate. The company had experienced nothing but growth since its founding in 1981, going from $1 million in sales to $27 million in a mere five years. The reality, though, was that this rapid growth had left us without a comprehensive understanding of how events occurring around the world could influence our small business, and we were about to be unmasked in a most public way.

As is often the case, once misfortune learns your address, more of it travels your way. Our largest customer was going through a leveraged buyout. The fallout resulted in a loss of $9 million in revenue in only 91 days. Our company was facing a pair of catastrophic events.

Literally, we bounced from crisis to crisis for a year. While constantly battling the fight-or-flight syndrome, we realized that we were mired in pervasive chaos, not because of our actions, but because of what had been done to us.

We ended up in Chapter 11 bankruptcy. When the company emerged from that experience, it was a shadow of its former self. Revenue was now $15 million, and our employee count had plummeted from 360 to 150.

Our team learned a lot from that experience, but what it boiled down to was this: to be successful in business over the long term, we must acknowledge that we do not have all of the answers, but that being grounded in principles allows us time to find the answers. Approaching business from this perspective creates hope among employees.

This concept holds true in the business world because rarely do we find organizations that are focused on a higher purpose. Caught up in the numbers, many organizations are operating in pure, unadulterated chaos because they have no idea what they do not know. They may not know a simpler way to focus on business. They may be blissfully and dangerously unaware that many of their people are not engaged in the company's mission and vision at a high level.

If this describes your company, and you are the leader, look no further. The blame most likely resides at your doorstep. Many leaders manage without leading. That is, the leaders simply do not have the skills or the tools to help their people focus and engage. The process is simple, but it takes time, and it can only be done one day and one relationship at a time.

The Chapter 11 experience that adplex suffered through was humbling, yet it was also liberating in ways that we never imagined. We learned that we were not nearly the perfect company our senior leaders thought we were.

Chapter 11 changed our lives substantially. It was the catalyst for what became the 4Ps Management System. We needed structure and organization. We needed meaningful goals and controls in the proper context of that system.

In retrospect, we came to define chaos this way: any dysfunction in the workflow, in the communication chain, or in the principles of the company. Chaos is counterproductive workforce activity that is ignored by management.

In today's business climate, companies need leaders who are willing to lead with vision. Without them, others in the organization will most likely establish their own direction, which can disrupt a company. Competing directions within a company create chaos, and leaders who do not clearly articulate their vision create confusion.

Chaos, then, is the absence of order and balance; it is an absence of principles and convictions. It is an absence of training employees inside the company and educating customers and partners outside the company. In essence, each of these diminishes stakeholder satisfaction.

Any organization today includes a diverse number of stakeholders. The impact, for example, of outside investors or private equity has created an unrealistic timeline for financial returns. Likewise, customers' thirst for low prices creates strain on the workforce as the firm tries to cut expenses. The result is undue pressure throughout the organization.

So, here are the questions: can we strike a balance between work and personal life in this pervasive chaos, and, if so, how do we do it? The answer is: as long as we lack a higher purpose, we cannot. Period. The truth is that there is really only one profession, one calling, and that is to serve God by serving others.

Whether we sell insurance, repair cars, perform surgery on people, or train horses, our profession is the same. This is an important concept—the idea that a doctor and a mechanic are actually in the same business, the business of serving others. Sadly, our culture denies this truth that all of us have the same purpose, regardless of educational background. This denial has serious ramifications that affect civilization.

For example, our obsession with attending college to have a fulfilling career has created the beginnings of a critical shortage of skilled craft workers. We are now seeing just the tip of the iceberg as a result of that misguided philosophy. As important as college is to some people, others who are not suited for college might make great plumbers, great carpenters, and great mechanics. Civilization needs people serving in these roles, and they, too, will find fulfillment in pursuing the higher purpose of serving and enriching the lives of others.

26

Perhaps we need to be reminded that 16 of our nation's 44 presidents never graduated from college. But those presidents came along before formal education became so crucial, you say? Well, let us fast-forward to a few names that might be more familiar.

Surely everyone knows by now that Bill Gates never finished his college degree, nor did Michael Dell, Ray Kroc, Dave Thomas, Henry Ford, Walt Disney, Thomas Edison, Mark Twain, Charles Dickens, or John D. Rockefeller Sr., to name just a few from a list of thousands.

If we were interviewing these people today, they would certainly stress the importance of education, and so do we. These examples are not intended to downplay the value of a college education; rather, they are designed to give hope to those who obtained their education in a less formal manner. Our society wants us to believe that not earning a college degree is the equivalent of a personal failure.

Let us be clear: intellect and education are two different things. A person can be seriously intellectual and not have a formal education. Conversely, in this age, a person can also be seriously educated and not have a hint of intellect. This is a sad commentary on formal education, but it should serve as a wake-up call to a brewing crisis—just another in a long list of issues contributing to pervasive chaos.

All of this is to say that the pervasive chaos in society and the workplace today is seen by a great, great many people as natural. The challenge is to recalibrate our thinking because this chaotic lifestyle is unnatural. This is not the way it should be. Regrettably, we have attempted to divorce what happens at work from what happens everywhere else. We cannot do that any more than we can divorce leaders from their spirituality.

One telling trend today is that more and more people are seeking fulfillment and meaningful experiences in nonprofits. Part of the reason that they cannot find this in the workplace is that we have convinced ourselves that qualities such as servanthood and selflessness cannot be experienced on the job.

The flaw is that many people think we have to go somewhere else—such as church—to get that sense of significance. Sadly, we have compartmentalized our lives. We have work, church, extracurricular activities, and social causes, and we pretend that somehow they do not go together. Many people have failed to embrace this truism, first espoused by poet and author Khalil Gibran: work should be love made visible.

We can begin by embracing this one-profession idea of serving God by serving others and decompartmentalizing our lives. This is essential if we are to create order and balance. Without a higher purpose, we will constantly chase whatever appears shiny today. We will never find the fulfillment, never find the peace, and never find the satisfaction that we all long for day to day.

Such tranquility will be similarly elusive upon retirement. If we fail to deal with chaos today, we may not have a retirement.

Economically, most of us will not experience a traditional retirement because times have changed. Either we deal with the chaos now to restore order and balance, where peace exists, or we will never find it. When we can no longer work, the icons of success will not all mysteriously appear for us so that we can enjoy those senior years. Those days are gone—if they ever existed.

If we have not figured this out, prepare for this bit of hard teaching: people will have to work well beyond what was once considered retirement age. The days of people retiring at age 55 after working for the same company for 35 years and living comfortably on a company pension into their late seventies are over. For those who are thinking about outliving the chaos, it simply does not work.

What is needed today is leadership—great leadership. A company's vision is only as strong as its leadership. Too many leaders today are afraid. They are paralyzed by the numbers. They might have a bold vision that will take their company into uncharted territory, but they refuse to be bold. They are quiet, and that loud silence is a breeding ground for continuous chaos and ultimate disappointment.

Leaders have to call people to action, and that can create conflict because it is not easy to do. In fact, it is painful because it is not comfortable. But if leaders are to realize the potential of their organizations and their talented employees, it must be done.

So, let us revisit the three-word title of this chapter.

Real pervasive chaos? Absolutely.

Chaos is unnatural and certainly destructive, no matter what anyone thinks.

PUNCH LIST

❋ In its simplest definition, chaos is any dysfunction in the workflow, in the communication chain, or in the principles of the company.

❋ The notion of long-term interdependence—a secure career marked by a mutual need between employer and employee—is all but gone.

❋ Many people are frightened to think of a world consumed with disorder and marked by self-centeredness, but we are moving in that direction organizationally and personally at breakneck speed.

❋ We are increasingly drawn to activities that are marked by a new, contemporary type of socialization—one that advocates self-interest above the common interest.

❋ Companies would be more capable of overcoming chaos and restoring order if their leaders had a reasonable approach to leading, one that includes a balanced perspective on business and a solid grounding in faith-based principles.

❋ A company's vision is only as strong as its leadership.

31

"The supreme accomplishment is to blur the line between work and play."

—ARNOLD J. TOYNBEE (1889–1975)

CHAPTER 2

CONTAINED PASSION, REGRETTABLY

Just as life was not designed to be chaotic, the passion within each of us was not designed to be contained. However, for most people today, passion unfortunately resembles a dying ember more than it resembles a raging fire. In fact, most people are so out of touch with their true passion that it would surprise them to learn that they ever had one.

The good news is that everyone has a passion. The bad news these days is that almost everyone's passion is nothing more than a hidden dimension of his or her personality—a secret unknown to organizations, their leaders, and often, even the person's peers.

Why are so many people today devoting so much of their precious time to pursuing passionless work? Certainly, the social mores found inside organizations are not helping. In fact, the parochial workforce system itself can dampen people's fervor. Marcus Buckingham, bestselling author and former researcher at the Gallup Organization, agrees.

In his book *Go Put Your Strengths to Work*, Buckingham suggests that far too often people conform to the demands of the world instead of listening to the voice within. Buckingham wrote:

> Back when you were young, your strengths were to be trusted. You felt your yearnings and your passions intensely, and they fueled your innocent belief that the world was going to wait for you, until one day you would emerge from your home or school, and you would get to make your unique mark on the world. And, then, somehow, sometime between then and now, your childish clarity faded, and you started listening to the world around you more closely than you did yourself.

While Buckingham's observation reminds us that we all once possessed a sense of joy and excitement about certain activities, his research tells us that few people really seek to keep passion's flame alive. It is important to know, however, that contained passion affects organizations every bit as much as it does people, perhaps even more.

In fact, research focused on the American workforce and released in 2007 by the University of Chicago indicated that 86 percent of workers were satisfied with their current job. In contrast, only 4 percent said that they were very dissatisfied with their work.

So, if almost nine out of ten people are happy with their work, what is the real problem? Well, the quandary resides in the area of potential—in not knowing what we do not know. While it may be true that nearly nine out of ten workers indicate that they are content with their work, the members of that same group are eager to point out that they live for the weekends or the periods when they are not working.

In other words, we have a workforce that is largely made up of people who are working not to pursue their passion so much as to pursue a paycheck. As one bumper sticker suggests, "If work is so terrific, how come they have to pay you to do it?" For millions of people, the phrase "joyful work" is an oxymoron. Much of today's workforce is not remotely acquainted with the concept. As a result, employment is often regarded as nothing more than a necessary evil, which is why we hear work referred to negatively too much of the time. The song "Take This Job and Shove It," written by David Allan Coe and made famous by Johnny Paycheck, captured this sentiment when it became a hit more than 30 years ago.

So, imagine for a moment that you are the leader of an organization, and you are charged with maximizing the potential of your workforce. As you assess your team, you realize that nine out of ten of your workers are desperately trying to survive the week so that they can enjoy the weekend. The one person who is not desperately living for the weekend would prefer another line of work. What do you think? What sort of chance do you have of realizing the potential of the organization?

The odds are that no leader can succeed given such a dismal portrayal of the organization's team. But here is where things begin to change; what has thus far been a dark journey begins to show signs of light. Where Buckingham seeks to empower the worker, we seek an opportunity to equip the leader.

Both initiatives are worthwhile and serve to complement each other, but let us be clear: everything rises and falls based on leadership. Theoretically, an organization could be full of employees using their strengths throughout the workday, but incompetent leadership will result in failure ten out of ten times.

Employees have to play to their strengths, but not to the exclusion of other areas of opportunity. The people leading an organization have to be able to assess the employee base and determine a way to find the people they need to accomplish their goals.

While it might make sense to choose as a leader someone who is strong with people because the leader will be dealing primarily with people each day, we cannot exclude the other skills that are necessary to realize an organization's potential. To be a formal leader in most organizations, a person requires key operational skills and a solid understanding of finances. This is particularly true as individuals assume greater responsibility.

Perhaps the first step, then, is to help equip leaders with a greater understanding of the idea that passion comes from a wellspring of higher purpose. Surgeons, for example, do not have a desire to operate on people so much as a penchant for saving lives.

Likewise, carpenters do not have a desire to hammer nails so much as a need for building homes. At United Supermarkets, we do not have a desire to sell bananas so much as a passion for feeding our neighbors.

Leaders who are looking to spark passion in employees must identify a higher purpose that connects people to something bigger than themselves, something that leaves a lasting legacy. In return, a foundation based on common purpose gives rise to individual passion. Once this happens, the future begins to look different from the way it looked before because the organization is no longer simply accepting its present circumstances. Employees become vested in the higher purpose, and in doing so, they become builders, not custodians.

The concept of there being only one profession, one calling, as described in the first chapter, helps us visualize the power of enriching the lives of people through a life of service. If leaders embrace this concept collectively, then they place everything else in its proper context. For example, when leaders are giving direction, the first question they should ask is, "Are we being faithful to the vision of enriching the lives of other people?"

Serving others is the best way to discover personal and professional fulfillment. Service is the one vision that transcends industry, geography, and religious differences among human beings. Imagine for a moment a world full of organizations filled with people with a passion for serving others.

Imagine a culture that allows organizations to retain their talent, eliminate unhealthy turnover, and discover the power of ideas unleashed in a collaborative environment. What would return on investment (ROI) look like then? What would ROI in humanity resemble then? Just imagine.

Once an organization has a meaningful vision, the challenge shifts to mining the valuable ideas of the team and directing its members' passion in productive ways. Remember, empowering employees and unleashing their passion is a two-edged sword. After all, the concept of passion means many things to many people.

For example, people may be extremely passionate about their work, but they may not express that passion in the same way as their peers. It is part of a leader's responsibility to know and understand the differences among those who make up a workforce. Not everyone is able to outwardly demonstrate enthusiasm.

Whether contemplative or expressive, in their own way, people are most passionate when they believe that what they do contributes to a meaningful result. Regrettably, this type of connection does not happen routinely in the course of employment. Indeed, people often fail to connect with the vision of a higher purpose because leaders often fail to connect with people.

In short, passion is too often constrained, constricted by the leadership and the culture that it creates.

As we suggested in the first chapter, one primary culprit is simply the busyness of life today. Whether people are at their jobs or in their homes, the noise of life has a way of snuffing out our passion. This is a slow process that happens a little bit each day—if we allow it to do so. Like indifference, surrendering to this process happens over time.

Regrettably, the deterioration of a passionate workforce will almost certainly eliminate any opportunity for superior performance. Setting new standards for results requires an ardent workforce. In other words, leaders find it impossible to get superior performance without passion.

In today's prevailing business culture, leaders sometimes confuse superior performance with results that exceed past performance or results that surpass those of the competition. While these standards are common-place and may have some usefulness, they set the bar too close to the ground for organizations that are seeking to evolve into what they can ultimately become.

Leaders actually discover superior performance not by comparing performance to the past, but by carrying out the potential of the future. Just about any savvy businessperson can provide a stakeholder with a tactical ROI for a given quarter, but it takes more to achieve success while formulating a strategy for long-term victory.

Victory is accomplished by encouraging people to discover the power of their passion. Such efforts result in employees taking ownership of the processes for which they are responsible each day, creating an environment in which teamwork reigns supreme, surpassing even the leader's imagination.

But contained passion ferments naturally in any workplace culture. One reason is that people become fearful of making mistakes, fearful of standing out, and fearful of being seen as being outside the norm.

The challenge for leaders, therefore, is maintaining authority while encouraging the workforce to perform with passion. First, leaders must be humble. The best ideas do not always emanate from the top. Second, leaders must recognize that not every idea is a good idea—and that this is okay.

Unfortunately, many leaders are threatened by a passionate person who might have a bad idea. They are unsure of how to deal with these excited people, who sometimes develop concepts that might prove not to be workable or logical when all the facts are in hand.

The challenge is how to treat that person in a culture of respect and innovation while balancing the fact that not every idea that bubbles to the top is workable. Leaders need to understand that how they handle a situation will communicate volumes to the rest of the people throughout the organization.

At United Supermarkets, for example, some passionate store leaders decided that the most important thing was to have store guests get in and out of the checkout lanes as quickly as possible. This vision was fueled by their zeal to make the experience for guests the best, and now the quickest, one possible.

Driven by this vision, they began posting a list at each store showing the scan times for every checker in order from fastest to slowest. They were consumed with speed and with moving people through the checkout process, so, implicitly, the checker listed at the top of the list was recognized as the fastest. Conversely, the least effective checker was at the bottom of the list.

All anyone had to do was walk into one of our stores and observe the result. Literally, we had people slinging groceries because no one wanted to be ranked at the bottom of this ominous list. It was an example of passion gone awry.

The key, though, was not to chastise the creators of the plan and say, "Have you lost your minds? What are you doing? We are trying to build relationships here. We are trying to engage people in conversations, but we are giving them broken eggs while hurriedly moving them through the line." We had to remind our leaders of Ultimate Service, a cornerstone of our company's mission.

"How can we deliver Ultimate Service if we are not taking the time to talk to guests?" Rather, we had to say, "This desire for speed is important, but in pursuit of that, we cannot be unfaithful to our mission of developing relationships and delivering Ultimate Service."

We needed to measure this thirst for speed in a sensible way in light of this element of our mission. We did not need to post rankings on a wall because often it turned out that a checker who was among the slowest in the store was also building incredible relationships by interacting with people while checking out their groceries.

In fact, we recognized that many of our "underperforming" checkers had guests who refused to have their groceries checked out by another checker—a clear indication of the power of the relationships and trust that had been cultivated over time.

Had we approached that situation in what many would consider a more predictable manner and said, "Whose idea was this? Rip those listings off the wall. What do you think you are doing?" it would have dampened other potentially great programs or initiatives from this passionate group of people.

Leaders become passion assassins when they stomp on people's ideas.

Leveraging people's passion is a challenging balancing act. At adplex, we once confronted a problem in Denver concerning the quality of our printing. We kept making mistakes and producing poor products. We were getting phone call after phone call, and it was confusing to the senior leaders in Houston because top-quality products were the standard at that plant. The situation was requiring us to regularly spend extra time checking quality control.

We traveled to Denver and spoke to our plant manager, and we observed some of the poorest-quality work imaginable. Finally, we pinned down the problem to a certain shift and found the answer.

It took only one trip to the pressroom, where leaders had posted a huge wall chart designed to measure the speed-per-hour output of the presses. The printing plant had been averaging about 18,500 copies per hour, but the goal was 21,000 per hour, and the team that was able to reach that mark received a financial incentive.

Even though only a small amount of money was at stake, all of the pressroom shift teams reached that goal because they saw the ability to make more money at 21,000 copies per hour. In reality, adplex nearly lost its largest and most profitable customer because of that misguided quest for speed. It was a powerful lesson about mortgaging the company's long-term future for a short-term financial gain.

Similarly, in the Air Force's Undergraduate Pilot Training operations, safety was an understandable passion; it was a topic of discussion in virtually every preflight briefing, squadron meeting, and wing commander's call (a meeting of all personnel assigned to the base).

The Air Force had a program encouraging instructor pilots to report missions in which anything unsafe occurred. Typically, this involved putting an aircraft into an inadvertent spin—a maneuver that was considered an unsafe condition if it occurred without prior planning.

We needed a system allowing instructors to report unsafe circumstances without fear of retribution. The reports were important to ensure proper training for student pilots.

The leaders decided to locate a box containing the required forms next to the commander's office. The forms were to be filled out when any unsafe, inadvertent event occurred. Needless to say, airmen had limited passion about filling out the form and placing it in a box next to the commander's office.

Not surprisingly, the instructors submitted few, if any, forms. Once the leaders of the program realized the problem, they chose to move the boxes into the restrooms, where they placed one on the back of each stall door.

Once that happened, they started receiving input, and some highly effective training programs emerged as a result of that much-needed feedback. When instructor pilots were in the restroom, they could close the stall door, fill out a form, and genuinely say what a student did, what the aircraft did, and what action they took to avoid an accident—privately. This was the kind of meaningful information that leaders working in the area of safety needed.

From a leadership perspective, the key is to provide sound guidance in directing passion. Unguided workplace passion results in chaos. In the Air Force, pilots used to jokingly refer to this phenomenon as leadership with "all thrust and no vector." Passion must be channeled via order and balance. That is the only sure way to create superior performance.

Unlike the previous examples, in which passion was alive, albeit slightly off the mark, many companies experience no employee excitement or enthusiasm. In fact, the absence of fervor has become so common in society that human resources professionals have a new term for it— "presenteeism," something that occurs when employees merely show up, mark their time, and depart, only to repeat this unproductive cycle.

To become fully engaged, leaders must guard against indifference. They must connect with employees. They have to take control and give employees permission to have passion in the workplace. Yes, they have to harness it, guide it, and monitor it without squashing it (intentionally or unintentionally), but they must encourage it to flourish.

Too often, employees contain their passion for no reason other than that it is never allowed to thrive, and they pursue careers for the wrong reasons—sometimes for money, sometimes for family, and sometimes for no reason at all. In any case, pursuing passionless work can hinder employees from realizing the purpose for which they were created.

Have you ever wondered just how many people are in this boat? Gallup Poll studies suggest that fewer than 17 percent of people in the workforce are in a position that allows them to play to their strengths every day. If that is true, then there must be a correlation between that number and the number of people who are in careers that are not suited for their individual talents or that do not allow those talents to flourish.

46

Learning just how huge that number might be is appalling, but it must be compelling simply based on the number of people who live for the weekend or live for their vacation.

Again, leadership must accept its share of the blame. Some of this has to do with people feeling that they have to be in management to make their career worthwhile or that they have to be a manager to be thought of as bringing true value to the company. Regrettably, some organizations harbor ill will toward employees who decline promotions, even when the decision to stay put is driven by family considerations.

Some leaders become frustrated when they learn that not everyone wants a position of greater responsibility. But rather than get frustrated by such an apparent lack of ambition, leaders must accept the idea that some people are already realizing their passion in the job they hold. Sadly, leaders often push people to accept positions that ultimately doom their careers. Bosses eagerly promote people for what they have already accomplished as opposed to what they might accomplish in the future.

When this happens, people who are not remotely qualified move into management. They lack the people skills or they lack the organizational skills, but they conclude that this is where they can make a difference or make more money. Then, if they fail in their new role, they are stuck because no one wants them to travel backward, and management is stuck with an untenable situation.

Unfortunately, such circumstances occur too frequently. Leaders do those people a disservice and hinder their potential. Almost unforgivably, leaders contain their employees' passion.

PUNCH LIST

❋ Almost everyone's passion is nothing more than a hidden dimension of his or her personality—a secret unknown to organizations, their leaders, and often, even the person's peers.

❋ An organization can be full of employees using their strengths throughout the workday, but incompetent leadership will result in failure ten out of ten times.

❋ Leaders who are looking to spark passion in employees must identify a higher purpose that interests people in something larger than themselves, something that leaves a lasting legacy.

❋ Once an organization has a meaningful vision, the challenge shifts to mining the valuable ideas of the team and directing its members' passion in productive ways.

❋ Superior performance is actually discovered not by comparing performance to the past but by realizing the potential of the future.

❋ To fully engage and unleash the passion of the workforce, leaders must surrender the armor of indifference.

"Sooner or later, man has always had to decide whether he worships his own power or the power of God."

—Arnold J. Toynbee (1889–1975)

CHAPTER 3

CALL TO ORDER!

Nothing shapes a personal or organizational legacy as much as the power of choice. All human beings and organizations possess this inalienable right, yet too often they forget to exercise it. To restore order in a world of chaos, they must actively choose to do so, and they must do so wisely. Their choices must reflect their purpose.

If inspiration is what they need to recognize the power of choice, they need look no further than the conduct of those members of the U.S. military who were held captive during the Vietnam War. Physically trapped in a world of chaos marked by torture and inhumane conditions for almost a decade, American prisoners of war (POWs) relied on the power of choice to prevail over their captors.

Like so many others who overcame exceedingly difficult circumstances, the late Medal of Honor recipient Admiral James Stockdale once remarked, "I never lost faith in the end of the story. I never doubted not only that I would get out, but also that I would prevail in the end and turn the experience into the defining event of my life, which, in retrospect, I would not trade."

Admiral Stockdale's comment, spoken to author Jim Collins and recorded in the bestselling book *Good to Great*, reveals the power of personal choice in restoring order in a world of chaos. In Stockdale's case, he made the choice to rely on God, not on men, and in doing so he became a beacon of hope for other prisoners. While that single choice sustained Stockdale throughout his eight years of captivity, it did much more. Many prisoners of war credited Stockdale and his personal conduct with being the key to their own survival because the admiral made a choice in service of his purpose.

Under the most difficult circumstances, Stockdale's words led fellow POWs such as Charlie Plumb to consider four years of captivity as nothing more than "a major inconvenience."

What does this say to those of us who are living free today? What sense of obligation do we have to exercise our inalienable right of choice? Can we restore order to a world of chaos in the same manner as these heroic POWs? The answer to this last question is a resounding, "Of course."

But the more pressing question might be, "Do we *want* to restore order to a world of chaos?" As suggested in the first two chapters, many people seem perfectly content to surrender to the busyness of life. Intellectually, they all might agree that they have the power of choice, but do they really desire to exercise their right as a matter of practice? If they aspire to excellence, then they must radically alter the present culture.

Perhaps the best place to begin is with a conversation about purpose. How is it defined? How do you define it? Does someone else define it for you? In today's pop-culture-influenced world, too many people face a definition of purpose framed by others. While we have heard many stories from people involved in a wide variety of professions, consider this story shared by Russell Anderson, a former business partner:

> It had been a busy couple of days in New York City. I was a manager overseeing multiple offices for the largest brokerage firm in the world, and I was accustomed to rushing out to Newark at the last minute to catch an evening flight back to Texas. My meetings on this particular day had gone well, but I could not deny that the adrenaline rush of life in the financial world— the pride of accomplishment—all of that was fading. By all measures, I was in the midst of a highly successful career. But by the measure that matters, my own personal measure, I was questioning the future. I wondered where life was taking me and my wonderful family. As I settled into my first-class seat, I wondered if

what I had accomplished was really important in the grand scheme of things. I thought about where my attention, talent, and energy were focused. The final question that I verbalized inside my brain was the most difficult: was my hard work and devotion to career really making a difference? On the plane that day, a lovely lady from Buenos Aires, Argentina, sat down next to me. I had visited Buenos Aires just recently for business purposes, so I struck up a conversation about the city and her native country. Once that discussion was exhausted, she asked me what I did for a living. I explained that I was a manager responsible for over-seeing several offices of a major investment brokerage firm. Finally, after a short conversation, she asked a question that crystallized the long-simmering conflict in my life. Her simple question, after hearing my expla-nation of my duties and responsibilities, was, "So, you don't create anything?" I was speechless. I was confi-dent I had made something. I helped make money. I helped provide secure futures for people. I helped train new financial advisors to be more professional. All of this was true—I had made a great many things in my life. But, to all of these protestations, she asked once again, quite simply, "So, you don't really create any-thing, do you?" It was at that moment that I knew my life was about to change. The woman had pierced my heart—the very thing I had been willing to overlook during my desire for status, excitement, and financial wealth at all cost. On that evening, at 35,000 feet above the Smoky Mountains, I determined that my life priorities would change forever because purpose r overtaken career as the guiding beacon of my life.

This same kind of epiphany happens in the business world, also. Typically, the frame is provided by investors and venture capitalists who believe that success in the public markets is defined exclusively by quarterly financial benchmarks, such as internal rate of return (IRR) or earnings before interest, taxes, depreciation, and amortization (EBITDA).

These performance indicators definitely have merit; however, they fall short when it comes to assessing an organization's likelihood for long-term success. Reaching that destination is a challenge requiring engagement on the part of all stakeholders to produce order and balance. Of course, a company must have profitability to allow it to accomplish all of the great work its leadership team envisions.

To be sure, the cash must flow if a business wants impact in terms of helping society. No one is dismissing profitability. It is a necessary fact of any successful business model. But it is only that—one piece of the sustainability puzzle.

True success in the marketplace should be measured in terms of the impact a business has on humanity—a different type of ROI, one that brings all of the dimensions of human life into play. Business leaders should ask themselves if they have made a contribu-

55

he personal fulfillment of their people. Did the
s make a contribution to the social nature of the
munity? Ultimately, it all comes back to enriching
man beings.

This is the higher purpose, not looking at the
amount of money a company generates from its operations. Look at some of the wealthiest people in the
world today: Warren Buffett, Bill Gates, and Ted
Turner. They have discovered that despite their accu-
mulation of massive amounts of wealth, the only way
they will truly enjoy it is to give it away, and they have
set out to transfer their fortunes to others.

The truth of the matter is, people can reach this
point in their own way when they have accumulated
so much that they realize that the only way to find joy
and satisfaction and true success is to return it to better humanity in meaningful ways. That is the key. A
fully realized life boils down to this: do you aspire to
improve the lives of others?

If you accept that premise, then consider embracing this idea: the most admired businesses in the future
will be idealistic, committed to developing leadership
teams and talent in search of a new definition of success. The people building these organizations will have
different talents that complement one another, but
their life mission will be the same. They will have an
unquenchable desire to enrich and improve the lives
of others, and that mission will affect all aspects of
their lives.

Imagine the leaders of tomorrow saying, "We have many talents, but we have one purpose and one calling, and that is to serve God by serving others." The power of making such a choice could harness chaos quickly and radically change the world. In the same way that Admiral Stockdale's decision to choose faith saved his life and the lives of others, business leaders who choose God's plan over man's plan have the best opportunity to restore order in their lives and the lives of their followers.

Just imagine.

Just imagine a generation of leaders proclaiming a new objective, one that encourages, inspires, and, in the end, lets go.

Imagine leaders with one objective: to maximize their potential in service to Him.

Take a few moments right now and ask yourself what purpose looks like for you, your family, and your children. How will you know when you have discovered your purpose? And, will you know it when you see it?

For example, at United Supermarkets, we talk about what our purpose will look like in terms of the growth plan we have in place. We want to see our company grow as long as we can remain faithful to our vision and our mission. But the question becomes, "What is the purpose that comes with growth?" The answer in our case—and possibly in all cases—is that we can now influence more people in a positive way.

Growing simply for the sake of growing will not satisfy our appetite, either personally or professionally. It just cannot happen. But if we tackle growth from the perspective that it gives us the opportunity to advance our vision, our calling, our profession, the one thing we all share regardless of our talents, then we can find satisfaction, and we can experience fulfillment.

Consider it in this way: when we attend a funeral, what we see more and more is a celebration of the person's life. When we really step back and observe carefully, we find that virtually all of the spoken words were centered on that individual's influence on people. At United Supermarkets over the years, the funerals of some of our long-standing leaders have drawn friends and colleagues from all across the country.

Anytime someone who has been part of our operation for decades passes, we are talking about a legacy that has touched many people. When we attend the service, without fail we face the reminder of how many people in the organization today hold their positions because of the tools and training they received from that person. In short, we reflect on the investment that person made in the lives of others. The person's true legacy is the time and effort he or she contributed to enriching others.

What will our legacy be? Is it going to be about a certain number in a bank account, or is it going to be measured by the number of lives in which we invested and the people we enriched? That is something that comes back as one of the big questions we must ask ourselves. For what purpose am I here? What will give me fulfillment and meaning? Part of the calling is nurturing, encouraging, and mentoring others to find their own voice and discover their hidden talents.

A call to order requires leaders and leadership, not managers and management. ROI is a concept that is driven by managers. It gets back to the leaders-versus-managers mentality. As Warren Bennis once said, "Leaders do the right thing; managers do things right." Now, think about the difference. Leaders invest in people. They invest in the future.

Investing in the future may not guarantee instant monthly returns, but it does provide sustainability for the life of the business. Doing the right thing builds loyalty in people. It builds loyalty in customers. Doing the right thing builds a covenant relationship, a solemn agreement that is binding on all parties not so much because of the power of a contract as because of the power of a promise.

Leaders lift spirits and create energy throughout the organization. On the other hand, doing things right wins quality awards. Doing things right builds financial momentum. Managers tend to use resources, not create them. Almost by definition, they suck the energy out of people rather than infusing people with enthusiasm and vigor.

Most people dread talking with managers, while most people love talking with leaders. As strange as it might seem, but unsurprisingly, investors in today's business world typically want managers. Because those investors want a financial lift as quickly as possible, they prefer less future vision and more immediate execution.

Over time, that strategy loses velocity. The workforce will experience a disconnect. Leaders avoid this entire sequence when they understand how to build teams. True, they must also pay attention to trends in the marketplace in terms of technology and consumers' purchasing decisions. Consumers have insatiable appetites, but only on their terms. True leaders always will be driven first and foremost by people.

Understanding this on a consistent basis is one way to develop sustained profitability, but it takes time, patience, effort, and consistency. Often, this runs counter to the investors' wishes. They prefer to focus more on selling whatever it is they have to sell to create a greater ROI. In turn, that allows for faster EBITDA growth. Companies are sold based on multiples of their EBITDA, so managers who can produce that growth are seen most favorably in the system.

It is not a question of rights. For example, in the case of adplex, the investors had every right to replace the leader with a manager after their purchase of the company. The investors owned 70 percent of the organization, and they had a different perspective on why companies exist. They felt then, as they feel today, that the only purpose of a company is to make money. Our view differed.

Yes, we wanted to make money as well; however, we felt that the purpose of a company was to influence people in a positive way. Likewise, we felt that the best reason to grow was to influence more people. But investors look upon growth differently. They typically see growth as an ROI issue. They want a return of a four or five multiple each year. We felt that business should be about much more than that. We were looking for ROI, both financially and emotionally, in the people of our organization.

Rather than seeing it as a return on financial investment, we thought of it more as a return on investment in humanity (ROIH). They both require people, but in the ROI case, people are seen as just another asset, equal to or less than the hard assets owned by the company.

Astute business leaders might want to take a look at a new P&L statement, one that has the purpose of refining and defining the values they place on the human aspect of the operation and how those stack up against hard assets such as real estate, stores, and fixtures.

In the end, the adplex investors made the right call, if their desire was to grow EBITDA by eliminating costs and driving sales to find a balance that elevates EBITDA as quickly as possible. The cost, though, is a loss of leadership and vision, neither of which can be outsourced or recovered quickly.

Many investors believe that they can hire a consultant to develop and implement a company's vision. They hire a high-priced consultant who walks in, looks around, and tells the managers where they need to go to reach their financial targets. Then the consultant leaves town. Let us be clear: leadership is the only thing that can deliver a vision. It cannot be bought, it cannot be outsourced, and it cannot be delivered by someone outside the company.

Leaders are the only ones who provide vision. How important is this understanding? To believe otherwise is the equivalent of saying that you will receive your salvation from the preaching you hear each Sunday. It is really the difference between religion and relationship. Our spiritual life is not about religion; all it does is put our relationship in context with the right elements. It does not create the relationship. People create the relationship as humans and make a conscious choice to begin a relationship with God, but they cannot outsource their salvation.

For example, imagine a company that is trying to outsource its vision. The consultant comes in with this great idea: the next level of technology or the next incredible product. Who is going to sell this idea to customers? Who will be the evangelist, convincing customers that not only does this organization have a great vision, but it also has the track record to overcome adversity if and when it occurs? Vision does not equate to an absolute.

Vision is perspective. It is a horizon, and we never know what is over the horizon until we make the journey. The ability to adjust to the changes in the market is often the difference between the survival and the collapse of an organization. It cannot be done unless a visionary is at the helm. A visionary knows how to make adjustments before it is necessary to make them.

Supermarkets are an interesting field of study when considering the power of relationships. Most independent supermarket companies rely heavily on the interaction between the customer and the checker because that one relationship has the power to make a customer feel comfortable and positive about returning.

Once an independent operation is sold to a company that is interested in consolidation, investors often shift the focus to synergies, operational performance, and total store count. In other words, the dialogue moves from one of building relationships with guests to one of labor savings by management. The new conversation is likely to be about taking every dollar possible out of the store in order to get more margin out of every dollar sold—all done in the name of efficiency.

Efficiency is the only context that the consolidators have because numbers are the easiest language to speak. If they look at the workforce inside their own organizations, they rarely celebrate and promote building relationships with people. They move to the next deal for the next dollar, and the entire context revolves around the ROI.

Leaders must recognize that organizations have many stakeholders. The constant clamoring from investors may be louder than the groans of others, but all voices deserve recognition for their importance. This is the beauty of balance and the power of collaboration.

All this focus on efficiency prompted one business owner to joke, "I can imagine one of these numbers guys attending a symphony. My guess is, he would be so obsessed with the fact that there was duplication in the strings section that he would never hear the beauty of their collective sound."

Several years ago at adplex, one of our financial partners bought out another investment group, and the company was rapidly sinking into debt. The company needed an infusion of capital, but our ardent pleas fell on deaf ears for months.

Even so, we went to work; within four months, we had totally restructured the company's assets, which required selling manufacturing plants without paying a single fee. We were able to move a significant amount of debt off the books and turn around the operation without any assistance from outside brokers. As soon as we had restored the organization's financial health, the new investors indicated that they wanted to make changes in the leadership team.

This seemed odd, given that the leadership team's work had saved the investors millions in commission fees, but they were uninterested in recognizing those efforts. It was a classic case of exploiting humans for their talents and then abruptly dismissing them once those talents were no longer appreciated in order to save money.

The call to order is doing the right thing. It is flying at the proper altitude, where leaders are able to see things for what they are and in their proper context because their perspective might have changed. A call to order should force leaders to question their own ability to hire correctly and surround themselves with talented people whose passion is in sync with their own expectations. That allows a leader to delegate. Once a leader accepts the idea that responsibility can never be delegated, but authority can, that leader will be very picky about who is hired.

Finally, a leader cannot play the blame game. It seems that blame is a constant in a society in which few people willingly step forward and accept responsibility. Look at the number of CEOs who have crossed the line, found themselves on the front page of the *Wall Street Journal*, and conveniently found someone else—anyone else—to blame. If a leader wants traction in the organization, the blame game must end. Exercising a call to order in this area of

65

business is every bit as important as exercising our power of choice in the other key areas discussed in this chapter.

A call to order is well within people's abilities, both individually and organizationally. In addition to mitigating the pervasive chaos and contained passion outlined in the first two chapters, it prepares leaders for proper implementation of the 4Ps Management System.

PUNCH LIST

❋ A call to order requires leaders and leadership, not managers and management.

❋ Performance indicators have merit; however, they fall short when it comes to assessing an organization's likelihood for long-term success.

❋ Leaders must measure true success in the marketplace in terms of the impact a business has on humanity—a different type of ROI, one that brings all of the dimensions of human life into play: ROIH, a return on investment in humanity.

❋ Growing simply for the sake of growing will not satisfy our appetite, either personally or professionally.

❋ Leadership is the only thing that can deliver a vision. It cannot be bought, it cannot be outsourced, and it cannot be delivered by someone outside the company.

❋ A leader should not blame others; leaders must step up and accept responsibility.

"As human beings, we are endowed with freedom of choice, and we cannot shuffle off our responsibility upon the shoulders of God or nature. We must shoulder it ourselves. It is our responsibility."

—ARNOLD J. TOYNBEE (1889–1975)

CHAPTER 4

PEOPLE, HUMAN BEINGS

The order of the 4 Ps is crucial. People come first for good reason: they are the single greatest asset in any organization. Ask any CEO of any company: staffing is the single biggest challenge to long-term success.

To put this another way, all organizations seeking sustained success must embrace a people-first culture. Reluctance to do so will almost certainly result in an inability to realize the full potential of the organization; quite possibly, it could result in the outright demise of the business.

Leaders can begin transforming their culture by placing the highest priority on people. Begin with a few simple questions. What is the value of a human life? It may seem shocking, but in today's culture, the answer varies greatly. If people are speaking of their own lives or those of the members of their family, the value is almost certainly incalculable.

But what if the life is that of an employee or an employee's family? Is the value reduced by a lack of familiarity? Are human beings any less human because they look different or speak differently? Intellectually, people might agree that the answer to these questions is straightforward: "Of course not."

But what does our practice say about our intellectual argument? Morally, most of us accept the idea that people are exceedingly valuable, but when did the lines between morality and organizational success cross? Did they ever? Truthfully, they cross every day—sometimes many, many times daily. The problem is that many leaders have become so desensitized to the importance of morality inside organizations that they fail to see the value of human beings.

When leaders fight the undertow of cynicism and stand up for what they know in their hearts to be right, they gain something of intrinsic value: the respect and loyalty of their employees.

Consider this story.

Jeff Pleshek was one of the most talented, competent, and upstanding individuals we ever had the privilege of working with at adplex. He was a trainer with a knack for teaching our customers and employees how to use software.

But, after several years of stellar service, we noticed a change in Jeff's demeanor during an annual company Christmas party.

Someone saw the always-affable Jeff sitting at a table alone. He was absolutely pale. When we checked on his health, he told us that he had bitten through his tongue the night before. A follow-up visit to his family physician revealed that he had suffered a seizure, although he had no recollection of the event.

Hospitalization followed, and after only a short time, tests revealed a large tumor on the front of Jeff's brain. Even so, the initial treatment options were promising: a low-grade tumor that surgery could remove. Clearly, this would not be an easy operation to complete successfully, but doctors expressed hope that Jeff could recover fully.

Unfortunately, that original optimism turned to pessimism when the surgeons discovered an extremely fast-growing, malignant tumor, not the low-grade, benign tumor they had anticipated originally.

To their credit, the doctors performed an incredible operation to save his life. After surgery, Jeff awoke and asked how it went. The surgeon explained that the tumor was malignant. Jeff responded, "Let's do everything we need to do. You're the doctor. I'm a fighter."

Jeff was serious; he was a prizefighter in the sense that he did not allow his circumstances to keep him from pursuing what he loved most: working with people to enrich their lives. For a period of time, Jeff tried to fulfill his duties, serving clients as he had done so successfully prior to the tumor. We knew things were different, however, because the illness began to hinder his ability to focus on details.

Eventually, we learned that the cancer had returned. He had another tumor, larger than the previous one. While the doctors managed to remove much of the second tumor, the recovery was understandably lengthy, and Jeff had to go on disability.

As with most disability insurance policies, Jeff was required to enter a hospice facility. Suddenly, the members of Jeff's family were faced with mind-numbing decisions. Literally, they were going to have to put Jeff in a facility, and they were going to have to sell their car and their home to afford the move.

As leaders of the organization, we faced an all-too-common dilemma: Our company insurance would not cover experimental drugs, so Jeff was without badly needed financial assistance from the insurance provider.

Faced with the facts, the senior leaders at adplex met to consider alternatives. By the end of the meeting, we had decided that there was only one thing to do: bear whatever burden was necessary to help Jeff and his family through this crisis for as long as possible.

We called the insurance company and said that we would cover the costs despite the precedent. We informed our board of directors about what was happening and about the decision we had made. We told them that the company could absorb the expense, or we would find another way, even if it meant paying for it ourselves.

Initially, the board members asked all of the questions one might expect. They asked about financial exposure; they asked for other information pertinent to the case. But, after seeing the level of commitment from the leaders inside the organization, the people who worked with Jeff day in and day out, the board signed off on the company's taking care of Jeff for a limited period of time.

Based on the diagnosis and all the available information, we anticipated taking care of Jeff for three months, but he proved to be the fighter he claimed. He hung in there for nearly a year, and so did the company's support.

Finally, Jeff came home to die. We loaned the family a vehicle to transport relatives and visitors. We did everything possible as a company, including paying Jeff's salary the entire time. He never missed a paycheck for 18 months.

In this tragic situation, we all thought: if the same thing happened to one of us, what would we want somebody to do? No one wants to face the reality of a disability policy that pays 60 percent of their salary, resulting in their having to sell their personal possessions to gain admission to a hospice facility.

Was this a bad decision? The answer may not seem simple. Seen through the eyes of an investor watching the outflow of cash, it could have been a bad call. But seen through the eyes of the company's leaders, striving to do what was morally right, it was a good decision. Sure, others might have wished we had not done everything we did, but we were all reminded, once again, that on matters of morality, we had to ignore the naysayers and press on with what we knew was necessary.

Lives changed because of the way adplex responded to Jeff, his family, and their needs. The company leadership was modeling a people-first culture that employees found appealing. It created a covenant relationship with the people we employed, and that built a work ethic and a desire among members of the workforce to make the company successful—not just because they were drawing a paycheck, but because they believed in a higher purpose. They knew Jeff's story.

Jeff's story is illustrative of a leadership team's proper use of the 4Ps Management System. Recognizing each person's value, personally and professionally, is the first step in restoring order. It is useless to discuss process without first addressing the people who employ the process. Partners cannot exist if people are not creating relationships, and superior performance is unachievable without people being passionate about their work.

People are the foundation of the entire management system, and, therefore, people should always be the first concern of the 4Ps—the fulcrum upon which everything else balances. Were it not for people, the other three Ps would have no functionality, and any organization would suffer from the ensuing imbalance of a misguided application of the system.

As was the case with *Built to Serve*, critics of *Equipped to Lead* will argue that references to faith, people, and the need for a higher purpose cross the line from a book about leadership to a book about spirituality. This is a criticism that we are familiar with and wholeheartedly accept. In the same way that our critics see power, position, and money as inextricably linked to leadership, we see faith, people, and purpose as inextricably linked to leadership.

We also see power, position, and money as tempo-   75
ral, whereas faith, people, and purpose are eternal. In that regard, leadership and spirituality remain inextricably linked.

Regardless, seen from a business perspective, one could argue we are headed to the same destination: superior performance. Nevertheless, we differ dramatically on the route and routine used to get there. Our experience has taught us that people, beyond their intrinsic value as creations of God, ought to come first in today's knowledge-based business era.

As much of a cliché as it might sound, effective recruitment, training, and retention are essential to long-term success. Leaders must learn to support people through bad times. If they do, they create loyalty.

They cannot command that; they earn it through showing that they care. In return, leaders who do that inspire people who want to participate in the process.

Loyal employees will work well with partners and represent the organization in a manner that is best for it when it comes to articulating vision. Employees help maintain the proper functioning of companies.

There are few, if any, examples of organizations that have achieved *long-term* superior performance without making people the heart and soul of their governing principles. People are essential. Sure, automation has altered the manner in which work is performed today, but contrary to popular belief, leaders should never simply eliminate people through automation. Instead, leaders should use automation and technologies to deploy people in areas where relationships, creativity, innovation, and collaboration are central to success.

Look at supermarkets. This is an industry that is dependent upon people even though an enormous amount of work has become automated. Scanning products for purchase is just one example of computer technology automating a process. However, the technology does not eliminate the need for people. Rather, it allows more time for the person checking groceries to communicate with the customer—to build a relationship.

Virtually all organizations have been able to eliminate steps and processes to increase efficiency and competitive abilities, but we will never see a time when people are eliminated from the equation altogether. Nor should we ever desire to see that happen. Competing in a value-driven world does not mean that people are more expendable. On the contrary, the more commoditized things become, the more an organization's people can create differentiation in a crowded marketplace.

Even so, the elimination of jobs in the name of efficiency is a popular refrain in virtually all sectors of business, despite the reality that people should be part of the process. Perhaps if leaders spent as much money and as much time helping people use more of their untapped intellect, they would realize extraordinary results.

Consider for a moment the power of a people-centered culture that is obsessed with helping people tap more of their available brain capacity—an organization's performance could increase exponentially. The results would be staggering. How do leaders do that? How do they mine that rich vein of knowledge in our workers? For starters, leaders should stop treating workers like numbers, like a necessary evil of business.

Think about it this way. If we want our businesses to be places of realized potential, then we have to be willing to exercise our employees' brains. It might help to think along the lines of conditioning for sports. If we want to run a marathon, we must increase our endurance over time. Or, if we want to build muscle through weight lifting, we must fight the natural effects of the atrophy that comes with age by increasing the weight over time or increasing the number of repetitions to grow the muscle.

Over time, we discover that what was once a personal limit is really no limit at all. Once we begin realizing our potential, we begin to increase our energy level—we become more in tune with the way our body works and the way discipline brings order and balance to our daily routine.

In fact, when we push beyond the old perceived boundaries, we begin creating a different future, and our entire outlook on life changes. In short, we begin manufacturing a feeling of hope within our soul. The analogies hold true for business as well, though we rarely think of an organization as a living, breathing entity. The best ones are exactly that.

In a sustainable business model, we know that the front line drives the bottom line, and when we believe that to be true, there must be an investment in front-line employees. They are going to make a direct impact on whatever the process is and on whatever the company's deliverables are.

But company leaders seem to misunderstand that equation when they spend an inordinate amount of time trying to cut costs on the front line, even if it means sending work overseas. We forget that a loyal, energized front line delivers enviable bottom-line results. Read this next sentence slowly: *Show us an organization that is trying to succeed by cutting costs, and we will show you an organization that has lost its feeling of hope.*

That is an incredibly powerful statement.

Consider it from the supermarket industry perspective. Checkers and sackers have everything to do with customers returning to a store . . . and they have everything to do with customers never returning. Why? Checkers and sackers spend more time with customers than anyone else in the company, including management. Those front-line employees may be carrying out the tasks of scanning groceries or bagging groceries, but they are very much a part of the marketing department.

What they say and do shapes the brand and encourages customers to connect emotionally with the company. It is the same in any job sector. The receptionist could well be the most important person a customer deals with when calling the corporate office. The manner in which the receptionist answers and handles a call will speak volumes about a corporation's operations. While such personnel might not make the most money, they are central to the overall success of the organization.

We might be surprised to learn that quite often one of the entry-level positions in a TV studio newscast involves ensuring that the news anchor's script is feeding into the teleprompter properly. Should we think of that employee as merely a teleprompter operator? Or, should we think of that person as the employee who is telling the news anchor what to say?

While anchors typically sit with a paper backup on the desk in front of them, nothing can make an anchor look more unprofessional than a teleprompter gone wild. This is another example of an extremely important position that is often marginalized because it typically does not rank high on the pay scale—it does not hold up to the misguided notion of success popularly defined as power, position, and money.

The people issue is enormous for all industries. Despite the fact that our legal system has complicated the latitude of leaders to engage their people, it can still be done. It must be done. Understanding the well-being of employees—physically, mentally, and spiritually—is essential to realizing the full potential of an organization.

How do we get this done?

Consider this short list of tactical action steps, and then make deliberate efforts to implement them immediately:

1. Acknowledge that every employee is God's creation and therefore worthy of dignity and respect by everyone inside the organization—starting with you. Never allow the business of number crunching or the need to pore over spreadsheets to desensitize your emotional connection to human beings. Make certain every birthday and anniversary is celebrated inside the

organization. You have too many employees to pull this off, you say? Delegate.

2. Embrace the concept that long-term superior performance cannot be achieved without a genuine commitment to the physical, mental, and spiritual well-being of every employee. Reexamine budgets to ensure adequate funding of the internal marketing needs. We recommend that 50 percent of an organization's marketing budget be spent on making employees fans of the company. Market first to your own people, then to the public. Nothing fails like a slick ad campaign that is little more than a figment of someone's imagination. Be real. If you cannot pay off your claim with your own people, then it most certainly will not resonate with the demanding public.

3. Never begin a staff meeting with a financial report. Instead, always ask each leader in the room about people first. Reluctance to adhere to the order of the 4Ps will create cracks in your new leadership methods immediately. In our own staff meetings at United Supermarkets, we rarely spend more than five minutes talking about financial reports. On the other hand, we have spent as much as ten hours talking about people issues.

4. Schedule blocks of time during every week when you can leave your office and engage employees in their space. Face it: your corner office may be beautifully furnished, but it is anything but inviting to rank-

and-file employees. Ensure that your "open-door" policy actually means that your door is open. Adopt this practice: if the door is open, allow anyone to enter, but if the door is closed, do not tolerate interruptions except for emergencies. Make sure the door is not always closed.

5. Try beginning conversations with employees with a question regarding their personal interests rather than to a question regarding business. Ask about an employee's family. You may be surprised to learn that employees enjoy talking about their loved ones. Nothing will bring a smile to an employee's face faster than telling you what his or her children have accomplished.

Next, consider a more strategic change. Think about reengineering your current P&L statement to include an employee satisfaction ratio or percentage— a number that can have a high level of importance attached to it. At United Supermarkets, we use a methodology developed by the Great Places to Work Institute.

The institute polls employees, using a scale from 1 (low) to 5 (high), regarding their feelings about how well a company addresses five key areas: respect, credibility, fairness, pride, and camaraderie. In 2007, for example, United Supermarkets' nearly 10,000 employees were surveyed using the institute's methodology. The results showed that 92 percent of the workforce indicated that they felt that, taking all things into consideration, United Supermarkets was a great place to work. A high level of trust exists.

Think about the potential impact of such compelling information. Would stakeholders see reported earnings differently if those earnings were produced with an employee satisfaction percentage of 20 percent? Conversely, would the value of a company that produced great earnings while recording an employee satisfaction percentage of 92 percent surpass that of other, less engaged organizations? How would stakeholders feel about investing in such a company? The answer is obvious.

Imagine the potential impact on curbing turnover inside an organization. Retained employees deliver continuity and accelerate processes because of a high trust level. The potential savings—real dollars that could be reinvested in the organization or taken directly to the bottom line—are overwhelmingly huge. In the case of a 50-store retailer, the savings could easily be equal to the profits generated by more than half the stores.

Picture the smiles that a leader could bring to shareholders' faces if profits could increase 50 percent without any capital expenditures. All of this and more is available to properly equipped leaders today.

Regrettably, though, ineffective leaders repeatedly fail to capitalize on this potential. Instead, they are mired in the same old conversations regarding revenue, gross, labor, and a handful of other numbers-related topics. Implementing the 4Ps changes the dialogue, starting with your own organization. That is the beauty of the system: it is the same despite all the moving parts and people in other areas.

At United Supermarkets, we have implemented this language. When the senior leadership team meets, the chief financial officer will talk about people, processes, partners, and performance. That is her language, and it is the same for the chief information officer, the chief operating officer, and all the other officers.

The consistent aspect of this is that everyone and everything begins with people. If the people part is not right, we know where the rest of it is going. It works for us because the 4Ps is a consistent and common business language that everyone understands.

In summary, the problem today is that if leaders are not focused on people, what they have on their balance sheets is just a bunch of numbers, and the numbers at the bottom of that P&L statement can be manipulated; some businesses manipulate them regularly. The balance sheet provides only a snapshot of the business at a given time. It offers no context whatsoever concerning the status of the engine, which is the people who create the earnings.

Imagine treating our family this way. If we led our family the way ill-equipped leaders direct businesses, the health of our family would be measured by how much cash we currently have on hand. How wrong would that approach be? If that were the case, then basically every pastor, every missionary, every young college student, and every aspiring performance artist would most likely be written off. Portions of the entire workplace would vanish.

This is a totally unrealistic approach, but it is precisely the style of operation adopted by myopic business leaders. Everything is based on the current quarter . . . until the next quarter.

Now, back to the parallel involving families. We have a quarterly family meeting, and we notice that our child's geometry scores are not up to par. We review the performance and issue notice that the child might not be around here much longer because he or she is an underperforming asset.

Sound foolish? Regrettably, this is exactly the way we often treat people inside organizations. Most investors have never really been exposed to an environment in which the leaders truly care about their employees. Instead, they have seen employees as tools, pieces of a big puzzle that can be discarded because no covenant relationship exists—certainly not like that of a family.

Such misguided managers rarely ask who someone is. They typically just want a head count and a dollar benefit. That is the world in which they live. They would struggle with Jeff's story because compassion and business are seen as mutually exclusive.

85

The concept of a company standing up and taking care of one of its own because it is the right thing to do resembles something more like a foreign language than a sound business practice. After Jeff died, we heard from other companies that had watched what we did and actually thanked us for setting an example that ran counter to the existing culture. Because we had chosen to be different, adplex received credit for breaking a mold and giving companies permission to think differently about this kind of workplace issue.

The lesson learned is that it should not take a cancerous tumor for a company to meet the needs of a human being. If that is the only time we feel we can rise to the occasion and meet the needs of the people in an organization, then we have missed much of what we have to offer.

People deserve many things while they are under the care of CEOs. They deserve a career path. They need to know what their opportunities are if they are planning to stay and invest their lives in your company. They need to see a clear direction of where they can travel.

Too many companies today fail to provide an understanding of the next opportunity. Employees deserve to know the treatment they can expect. Answering these questions publicly sets the rules of accountability internally for those who lead.

When people come first, the organization and its success follow naturally.

PUNCH LIST

❊ All organizations seeking sustained success must embrace a people-first culture.

❊ People are the foundation of the entire management system, and therefore, people should always be the first concern of the 4Ps—the fulcrum upon which everything else balances.

❊ People, beyond their intrinsic value as creations of God, ought to come first in today's knowledge-based business era.

❊ Competing in a value-driven world does not mean that people are more expendable. On the contrary, the more commoditized things become, the more an organization's people can create differentiation in a crowded marketplace.

❊ Leaders should consider reengineering their P&L statement to include an employee satisfaction ratio or percentage—a number to which they attach high importance.

❊ A balance sheet provides only a snapshot of the business at a given time. It offers no context whatsoever concerning the status of the engine, which is the people who create the earnings.

"Apathy can be overcome by enthusiasm, and enthusiasm can only be aroused by two things: first, an ideal, which takes the imagination by storm, and second, a definite intelligible plan for carrying that ideal into practice."

—ARNOLD J. TOYNBEE (1889–1975)

CHAPTER  5

PROCESS: BLOCKING AND TACKLING

Everything that happens inside an organization is tied to a process. If we closely examine the architecture of every discipline within an organization, we discover a series of complex systems, some formal and some ad hoc, that upon deconstruction reflect an orderly subsystem of processes—a subsystem comprising inputs and outputs. Comprehending this concept helps us understand the important fundamentals of leading an organization.

Reflecting for a moment on great leaders of the past, no list of leaders devoted to blocking and tackling is complete without legendary football coach Vince Lombardi, a confessed stickler for executing the basics properly, every time. For this reason, Lombardi was known more as a highly effective motivator than as a successful innovator. He was quoted as saying,

"Some people try to find things in this game that don't exist, but football is only two things—blocking and tackling."

To underscore his point, Lombardi designed one signature play: the Lombardi Sweep, a running play in which the quarterback hands the ball to a running back who follows the lead blocks of at least two offensive linemen running parallel to the line of scrimmage. The Green Bay Packers used the play repeatedly during their dynasty years in the 1960s. The lesson is simple: if we execute the processes correctly, we can succeed regardless of what happens—even in the face of nitty-gritty competition.

When the Packers played, everyone playing or watching the game knew that they were going to run the Lombardi Sweep, but even so, the play was among the most difficult for opposing teams to defend against. Lombardi's team ran the play because he knew that its successful execution when the other team knew it was coming would build confidence in his players. It did. In just eight years as the Packers head coach, Lombardi's beloved team won five National Football League championships.

As leaders, we must ensure that the fundamentals are being executed flawlessly. In fact, if we could design the perfect process model, it would look like Figure 5.1.

FIGURE 5.1

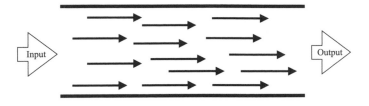

Projects, tasks, and initiatives would flow effort-lessly from input to output with absolutely no obstructions or hindrances. The process would be perfect, inasmuch as it is the model of efficiency. Of course, we know how difficult it is to attain perfection. More often, we discover that processes are inefficient, plagued by a series of pinch points that reroute effort and impede progress. The model in Figure 5.2 more closely reflects what happens in most organizations.

91

FIGURE 5.2

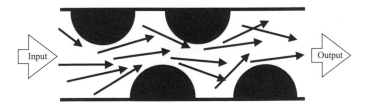

Process failure can occur anywhere and anytime senior leaders take the little details in any large project for granted. Such was the case a few years ago at United Supermarkets.

We wanted to improve the processes involved in building a new store—we had grown tired of expensive change orders modifying the plans. Using the logic provided in this chapter, these change orders seemed to be more a reflection of poor planning than of necessary revisions. So we attacked the problem by identifying the current process of building stores. We asked each person involved in new store construction and the people who actually worked in the stores to comment on the process from their perspective.

We started with an area that seemed to be causing the most trouble, both financially and practically: the food service/deli department. And we asked the users first, since the process seemed to be lacking their input.

We started with a simple question: "Why are we having so many change orders in the construction of these stores?"

Their response was telling. "There is no process."

We asked, "What do you mean, 'There is no process?'"

They said, "We're not involved in that."

Of course, that prompted another question: "What do you mean, 'You're not involved in that?'"

"Well, what happens is that the architects draw up the plan based on conversations with the business directors, and then we're told that we have to make it work," they said. "That's the way it works."

From the perspective of the users, we had "corporate executives" telling food service specialists how their departments should be configured and, in essence, operated. In our case, many of the executives making the decisions had not worked in the stores for more than a decade, and some had never worked in a deli. They all meant well, but we were creating problems—costly problems.

It was an easy diagnosis.

We had a process failure, and we needed to try something different. We opted to rent a warehouse and construct a deli using pressed wood, cardboard, and other inexpensive materials. And, before we took this step, we sought input from the users on which to base our three-dimensional construction. Beyond that, though, we invited the users to visit the mock-up and provide feedback regarding the efficiency of the layout.

The users' response was ecstatic because they had difficulties processing blueprints, even when they were consulted. The two-dimensional plans were almost like another language.

It was that kind of dialogue that created user-friendly and easily followed processes. As a result, on the first store we built after doing this, we reduced change orders by nearly 75 percent.

Just as importantly, we developed a better relationship between the users and the executives. Senior lead-

93

ers renewed their commitment to supporting these users, rather than the users having to fit into a plan. The process opened our eyes in a way that resulted in high trust, more collaboration, reduced cost, and better store efficiency.

It was a win-win-win-win situation because the people who worked in the deli owned the environment and were proud to be a part of it.

We have spent a lot of time dealing with organizational chaos and how it overwhelms the workforce. Part of that is a result of the complexity of what the great majority of employees have to deal with—day in, day out. A lack of engagement and investment is the result, and organizations end up with employees who are ill equipped to tackle the issues, simply because of the complexity and diversity of what is coming at them with frustrating speed each day.

We say all of this to deliver one truth: the beauty of understanding process is to say, "Look, this can appear to be as complicated as you want to make it, but it is nothing more than a subsystem of inputs and outputs."

If an organization can take its processes and break them down one by one (a tedious undertaking, to be sure), then it will discover that no issue is too complicated to comprehend. Few people can grasp 10,000 processes in one sitting, but it is possible to tackle a process-by-process review to discover what might really be an issue. The fastest way to resolve an issue is to involve the people using the processes.

Typically, those who are expected to use a process know that it is flawed before anyone else does. No doubt, people are resilient and ingenious, and they will figure out a way to circumvent a faulty process when that is necessary to accomplish a task. It happens that way often because the great majority of organizations are driven top down. In other words, someone at the top of the pyramid has created a process for people downstream to follow.

By all accounts, that defies logic. It would make more sense to include the people downstream as part of the process solution. Doing so will create buy-in from workforce personnel. Those who are expected to use it now have ownership in an effective and logical process because they understand the instructions and the reasoning behind it.

At United Supermarkets, the first thing we try to do when something is not working is bring in the people who own that process so that we can talk to them about why it is not working. As a result, in our monthly executive meetings, we include a front-line business director to talk about processes.

This occurs at every meeting without exception. A different department is scheduled each month throughout the entire year. That department leader is responsible for ensuring a meaningful dialogue that educates the senior leadership team.

We have used this process for the past four years, and it is amazing to hear an employee come in and talk about how well things are working and how much better they could be if a process change or two could be made. It is a way to fix something quickly, and it is also a way to remind the senior leadership team that if it is hearing about process failures in one department, it is likely that similar failures are occurring in other departments, as well.

This approach is a reflection of what is happening across the entire company. The message to the senior leaders after the meeting is to get into the stores and talk to people about processes to learn what is working and what it is not. Many of these processes are constricted, many are failed, and many are being circumvented. The only way someone sitting atop the organization will ever find out that something is wrong is when performance goes haywire.

Now, how is that for restoring order and balance? Things might be going well because of circumstances outside of your control. After all, many factors affect the numbers each day, and some of those factors are internal while others are external. It is possible you could miss this process breakdown altogether, and this could result in an oblivious senior leadership team sitting around high-fiving one another on an awesome quarter, when, in reality, the company is teetering on the brink of disaster.

A little process planning at the start can save a lot of money at the conclusion. It makes a huge difference. Good processes inspired by empowered employees create good results.

Good processes are products of good direction, and they must have strong leadership if they are to be developed, implemented, and championed. Good leadership gives people permission to analyze the processes. It should come as no surprise that the older a company is, the more embedded in history its processes are, and they become sacred cows that everyone fears to touch or even approach.

At adplex, we had had a customer service issue for a long time, and after looking into it, we heard that the process was one that we had started decades before. Of course, that process began when we had only one customer. At that time, with a single customer, a manual spreadsheet worked fine.

Decades later, though, our accounting people were still fighting the manual spreadsheets and making a number of errors because they thought there was a mandate to do it that way.

At last, we told them it was permissible to automate the process. Sound elementary? You might be surprised by how easy it is to get hung up in a historical pattern of an antiquated and ineffective process.

We once had a technology problem at adplex that led to a customer's being charged anywhere from $800 to $2,500 per week more than what it had expected. For that matter, it was more than we had expected, as well. It was baffling to us, so we started really focusing on the processes making up a rather complex billing system.

The customer told us that the problem occurred when ads were released to the public online; the files we were posting did not match the print ads scheduled for insertion in local newspapers. Because the files and print ads were different, our people had to go in and manipulate the Web pages manually every time to ensure accuracy.

Our people saw that as a customer issue, one that warranted a bill for the labor costs involved in correcting the problem. We called the customer to talk it through, and, not surprisingly, we were told we were wrong. We needed a face-to-face talk. Only after meeting personally could we grasp the problem.

We hit on a solution. Our people would enter the changes into their spreadsheet. We would do the update on Friday. This was a workable plan that would save the client as much as $10,000 per month in extra costs.

Resolving this one process issue exposed other opportunities to streamline the operation. For example, the customer also was experiencing problems with promotional signage for stores. The customer was upset about being charged for something, but the bigger issue was that no one had ever analyzed each process.

The issue emerged because of billing discrepancies, but it evolved into a systematic review of the processes driving the expense.

What we are getting at is that the quality of the outcome—the product or the service—is a direct reflection of the processes. If your processes are broken, misguided, or misaligned, you will end up with either a deliverable that is less than what you want or a deliverable that costs more than it should.

The fastest way to get traction within an organization is to take a deep dive into the processes being used because that is where the greatest potential for change exists. The reason is that in most organizations, the people who are using the processes each day are rarely consulted.

If you are an agent of change looking to alter a company quickly, consider these three questions:

- What is the workflow?
- What are the processes that make up the workflow?
- What do the users say about the effectiveness of those processes?

The military, which is a remarkable training example, embraces the logic expressed in process and workflow deconstruction. This was a teaching tool in the Air Force, particularly with pilots, to help them understand the mechanics of an airplane.

The military used an interactive training module that literally showed a drop of fuel that has been put into the gas tank on the wing, and showed that little bit of fuel moving through the check valves and through the boost pump to the engine, where it burned.

The exercise allowed pilots to better analyze malfunctions in flight. For example, if the boost pump warning light illuminated, pilots would be able to troubleshoot the malfunction in a logical manner because they understood the process by which fuel burned.

But, if you do not understand the process, you do not know the direction in which to go. That contributes to chaos . . . and crashes.

Another organization that has done a reasonably good job of understanding process analysis is the National Transportation Safety Board (NTSB). When this group assesses an accident, it takes it apart one process at a time. The NTSB's experience with accidents reveals a chain of events in which one link is broken.

Each link represents a process, and the chain is reassembled by going back and examining each link. The NTSB looks at the pilots, what they ate, what their social issues might have been, all the way from the beginning throughout the entire accident.

The NTSB implements a phenomenal methodology, but it goes through this because it is the only way to get to the root of the problem. Too often, leaders do not want to go through the analysis. They think it takes too much time. It is too much of a grind, so it becomes more convenient to deal solely in generalities.

Too often, the result boils down to the personality. It becomes the fault of a person, when, in reality, it is the process that keeps the person from succeeding. People leave organizations far too often because the leaders fail to do the hard work, take the deep dive, and collect the necessary data. Put another way, too often leaders fail at the fundamentals—the processes, the blocking and tackling.

Let us return to the gridiron for one last football analogy. Take a football team and isolate one specific play to illustrate this point. The play represents a workflow. It has a beginning and an ending. A subsystem of 11 processes takes place with each snap of the ball.

Teams film their games to analyze each process in the workflow and understand why a play did not fulfill its objective. In the case of a play that does not succeed, it could be a poor execution of any one of the processes. When a play succeeds in a touchdown, typically all of the processes succeeded as well.

In this analogy, the input is what each player has been assigned to do on that play. The output, if it succeeds, is that the other team's defenders will not tackle our runner. The workflow is how many yards they expect. Maybe the play is designed to gain ten yards, or maybe it is designed to produce a touchdown. Either way, that is the workflow.

In the simplest terms, something is given to someone; that person does something with it and turns it over to someone else. That is input, process, and output. Everything we do is a process, and a great process requires collaboration. You must have high trust and an emphasis on humanity, or you will have blame and frustration, which leads to more chaos.

Finally, remember that no process is unimportant. You can take something as critical as sending a rocket into space and all of the complexity of the engineering and the rocket and the fuel and the people and the training, but guess what? With a faulty O-ring, disaster looms. It is often the tiniest things that cause the biggest problems.

Efficient, streamlined processes bring order and balance to chaos. Properly equipped leaders know just how true this is.

PUNCH LIST

✳ Processes often are inefficient, plagued by a series of pinch points that reroute effort and impede progress.

✳ Organizations end up with employees who are ill equipped to tackle the issues simply because of the complexity and diversity of what is coming at them with frustrating speed each day.

✳ Those who must use a process know that it is flawed before anyone else does.

✳ Good processes are products of good direction, and they must have strong leadership if they are to be developed, implemented, and championed.

✳ The quality of the outcome—the product or the service—is a direct reflection of the processes. If processes are broken, misguided, or misaligned, the result will be a deliverable that is less than what is desired or a deliverable that costs more than it should.

✳ People leave organizations many times because the leaders fail to do the hard work, take the deep dive, and collect the necessary data before taking action.

"Compassion is the desire that moves the individual self to widen the scope of its self-concern to embrace the whole of the universal self."

—ARNOLD J. TOYNBEE (1889–1975)

CHAPTER  6

PARTNERS: HUMAN BEINGS, TOO

R elationships are the only real currency that matters. Effective leaders must understand the power
of this statement, and they must make the proper
application of its teaching. For example, customers
and vendors should be recognized for what they are:
partners in the success of any organization. Sadly, the
rapacious behavior found in the prevailing business
culture today is destroying partnerships, not building
them.

Rather than looking for ways to progress together,
many titans of industry resort to mandates, edicts, and
ultimatums. Regrettably, the great majority of so-called
advances in business these days, including enhanced
profitability, come at the expense of partnerships.

Rest assured, this is not a good thing.

In the context of the 4Ps, *partners* actually refers to all external stakeholders. In other words, customers and vendors, along with communities and outside investors, must receive the same care and feeding as people working inside the organization. The relationship between this diverse group of external stakeholders and internal employees is one of interdependence—neither group can thrive without the others.

Why, then, do so many organizations engage their partners not in a spirit of cooperation, but in a spirit of antagonism? Clearly, many organizations cannot embrace the notion of interdependence because their judgment is negatively affected by pride. This is especially true among organizations that are driven by people who believe they are overachievers, capable of intimidating anyone else in the marketplace because of their size or market share. This absence of any humility leaves them unreceptive to history's painful reality, summed up so succinctly by Arnold J. Toynbee: nothing fails like success.

Like Roman conquerors, some of the largest companies in the world act as if they have command and control of everything. They fail to heed the warning that all glory is fleeting. Dr. Laura Nash, in her book *Believers in Business,* quotes former Secretary of State James Baker:

"Someone asked me what was the most important thing I had learned since being in Washington. I replied that it was the fact that temporal power is fleeting." Baker went on to observe that once driving through the White House gates he saw a man walking alone on Pennsylvania Avenue and recognized him as having been Secretary of State in a previous administration. "There he was alone—no reporters, no security, no adoring public, no trappings of power. Just one solitary man alone with his thoughts. And that mental picture continually serves to remind me of the impermanence of power and the impermanence of place."

Long before Secretary Baker's epiphany, the Apostle Peter put it this way: "All men are like grass, and all their glory is like the flowers of the field, the grass withers and the flowers fall, but the word of the Lord stands forever." Even so, many ill-equipped leaders defy these realities, opting instead to demand that vendors change the workload, change the way in which products go to market, and help pay for those changes. In return, they promise to bring other partners to the table to share the financial burden before distribution takes place, but their word means nothing.

As a result, all stakeholders suffer. In the case of the vendor-partners, they routinely feel overwhelming pressure to lower their prices. They regularly face demands that they figure out how to reengineer their companies to provide the same product at a lower cost than that of a year ago. A year from now, guess what? The demands will be the same, including one to reduce costs even more. What ensues is tragic. People are relegated to a position of unimportance. Partnerships dissolve. Chaos prevails.

At best, diffident leadership perpetuates a vicious cycle that forces the export of jobs and compromises the quality of goods and services. At worst, irresponsible leadership knows no boundaries in pursuing profits. Yet, it happens—every day and at an alarming rate.

What ought to be a partnership fueled by a spirit of collaboration too often results in nothing more than a procurement exercise—an emotionless application of numbers. It is a method of conducting business that is devoid of humanity.

Properly equipped leaders know better than to subscribe to such methods. Instead, they build loyalty to their company among suppliers through the way they treat their vendors. They engender an enormous amount of positive feelings toward their company because vendors are treated like partners. That results in high-quality work and a long-term win for both parties.

Such loyalty cannot be adequately valued on a spreadsheet, but the importance of developing partnerships is undeniable. That above-and-beyond loyalty has benefited United Supermarkets, as well. For example, if a large storm hits West Coast produce suppliers, we enjoy the kind of relationship with the growers that are our partners that means that they provide us, literally, with the last of what they have instead of giving it to one of the large consolidators in the marketplace. That is the power of relationships.

A relentless pressure for lower prices, however, is commoditizing basically everything that is not highly differentiated. The current system of procurement is extremely challenging for partners, and it has driven companies of all sizes to aggregate their volume in order to price competitively in the marketplace.

The aggregation process can be a slippery slope because in most cases it is taken outside the organization and placed with a third party—a staff of procurement experts. When this process is done poorly, these people conduct the negotiations with little input from the company, especially regarding preexisting relationships.

Organizations that embrace this type of business method suddenly find themselves unwittingly tolling the death knell of meaningful partnerships. Lost in the noise of temporary savings is the cost of long-term relationships.

Looking at this issue closely will reveal a dilemma that companies face constantly. Imagine that you have a supplier who has been with you for more than 50 years. This supplier is not big enough to handle the aggregated volume that you need for your business if you are to get the price necessary to attract customers. But the supplier has always responded to your need. He has always been in your court. So, how do you preserve this valuable relationship while gaining the benefits of aggregated volume?

Some third parties get it right. For example, Topco, a food industry co-op, employs a team of procurement professionals to assist its members in aggregating volume on items not for resale to customers. The program, called TopSource, takes a much different approach to procurement.

Topco prefers to involve the incumbent supplier in the process, and it often helps facilitate growth for companies that are not prepared to meet the expected volume. TopSource employees value relationships developed over time with member companies. Whenever possible, they seek to retain good suppliers while aggregating commoditized supplies.

A good example of this can be found in printing. Most companies utilize regional or local printers to print their weekly advertising inserts. In many cases, the size of the company placing the print order means that multiple printers are needed to provide the necessary total volume. In other words, no one printer can accommodate a retailer across a nationwide footprint, so various printers do the work.

To meet the demands successfully, representatives of the retailer or its designated procurement experts look at what printing plants have in common. The answer is paper. Sometimes the sheer volume of the paper required can result in a huge expense. For example, paper costs can represent as much as one-fourth of a $10 million advertising budget.

A professional procurement team can make a profound difference by making the paper purchase centrally and arranging shipments directly to regional printers. This process keeps the regional players in the game, allows them to maintain their relationship with the retailer, and provides the benefit of aggregated volume.

This can be a little more work, but in the end it preserves the relationship—the kind of partnership that allows you to call in the middle of the night if a problem occurs. Such partnerships are wonderful because they are built on human beings working with human beings to accomplish a mutually beneficial task. Tell those partners that you have a problem, no matter when, and they will work to help solve it.

For example, from time to time, whenever you are dealing with partners, errors will occur. At adplex, we were in the business of printing newspaper circulars. It was a high-stakes game because one tiny mistake could prove extremely costly.

Years ago, a customer of ours sent a fax to our printing plant indicating that it needed to make a ten-cent-

111

per-pound increase in fryer chicken. The fax indicated that the customer also wanted to change the brand from one leading seller to another. Regrettably, however, no one called to let us know that the fax was being sent, and the communication went unnoticed during a break at the plant.

We ran hundreds of thousands, maybe even millions, of promotional circulars featuring deep discounts on chicken legs and thighs. This occurred during a holiday weekend. The advertisements appeared in newspapers distributed throughout the southeastern United States. Unaware of what was about to happen, we went about our business of ensuring acceptable quality for the printing. We tracked the outbound shipments to ensure that the ads would arrive at the respective newspapers on time.

Then something bad happened. The advertising manager for the retailer called and asked if we were standing up or sitting down. He told us to sit down.

"We've got a problem," he said. "We're $38,000 upside down and going the wrong direction fast. We've got this ad today, and chicken is moving like crazy in the stores. We're off by 10 cents per pound, and it's the wrong brand."

"How on earth did it happen?" is about all we could manage to say. At the time, we knew very little about what had gone wrong, but we offered this solution to an understandably panicked advertising manager. We said, "We're good for it. We will cover the costs of the mistake at the retail price. Period."

We all watched in horror as the tab grew throughout the weekend. What had initially been $38,000 was growing—$68,000, $89,000, $110,000. We called the customer and asked, "Is there anything you guys can do to mitigate this for us? We are committed to making good on this, but we need some help."

The customer agreed to remerchandise the product in order to downplay the promotion. It was a clear example of a partner trying to help. Remerchandising meant contacting hundreds of stores. Fortunately for us, it worked. Sales peaked, and the tab ended up being $128,000. We flew to North Carolina, talked to the customer, and handed over a check for that amount.

As a result of this partnership performance, the customer called the following week and signed a three-year contract. The business relationship also grew in volume. Our revenue with the customer increased from $3 million per year to $24 million per year.

Now, here is the rest of the story.

The contract between our companies required any changes to be both faxed *and* phoned to our manufacturing plant manager. We discovered the fax, but the customer never made the call to alert our manager to the last-minute change. Our legal staffer said, "We can get out of this $128,000 because this was just faxed, not called in." But we had covered it, and that was all that mattered to us.

The next time we were in the customer's offices, though, we made the advertising manager aware of the contractual agreement. He admitted to making the mistake, and he nervously asked what we wanted to do about it. We told him that the situation was taken care of; we just wanted him to know that it was not entirely our problem.

The advertising manager understood that, and he appreciated our handling of the matter. It removed a lot of pressure from him and his people because an error of that magnitude was going to result in serious consequences.

That is what partners do for each other. They support each other during good times and bad times. When a true partnership exists, invoices are paid immediately and without spending a lot of time scrutinizing each line. Properly equipped leaders believe that treating vendors like partners creates a high-trust relationship. If a mistake occurs on an invoice, leaders of both organizations know that it will be resolved fairly.

If we trust a partner, we can proceed much further than if we are constantly second-guessing each other, constantly reviewing each invoice line, constantly wondering about agendas and motivation. It is good busi-

114

ness. And what if a last-minute project develops and a vendor-partner is needed to accurately complete the work? Which vendor will you want to have handle the important project? Will you choose the lowest bidder, some vendor-partner whom you have never met?

Or, will you choose the vendor-partner who has brought value to the organization and in whom you have long-standing trust, but who might charge slightly more? Which provider do you select? Do you select the lowest price or the highest trust? Companies choosing high trust as their method of conducting business realize extraordinary partnerships. No vendor-partner in his right mind would breach that kind of trust with a company.

Unfortunately, the prevailing culture is stuck in a haze of confusion when it comes to the treatment of vendor-partners. Organizations spend countless hours, wasting person-years of time, chasing insignificant minutiae, and they do it with little or no dialogue with people.

A better approach is possible. Vendor-partners understand the need for lower pricing and can offer recommendations on ways to realize reduced costs. All that vendor-partners want is the opportunity to be part of the dialogue—a part of the team that is formulating the solution. Vendor-partners must make a profit. It is in every stakeholder's interest for the vendor-partners to make money. Otherwise, organizations find themselves constantly having to educate a new crop of suppliers. Lost in the exercise are business continuity and the value of lessons learned by long-term partners.

Consider this sage truth that every vendor-partner knows: it is always easier to get the business than to keep the business.

Why? This seems counterintuitive, right? Well, most organizations forget this fact, if they ever knew it at all. Only one company knows the actual costs associated with servicing a customer, and that is the incumbent. Regardless of what the specifications outlined in the request for proposal (RFP) said, the cold, hard truth regarding what it takes to execute the RFP's deliverables properly can never be fully known by a company entering from the outside.

Therefore, when decisions are predicated on price and price alone, the incumbent is always at a disadvantage. Ill-equipped leaders fail to connect these dots. As a result, organizations churn vendor-partners like Breyer's churns ice cream—minute by minute.

What is the cost of churning partners? What is the true cost of subscribing to a misguided notion that in every negotiation with a vendor-partner, someone has to lose? A little humility goes a long way. True vendor-partners will always approach their business from one perspective: is this the right thing for the cus-

tomer? If it is the right thing to do, a true vendor-partner has an obligation to tell the customer this, even
when the news reduces his profit. It may come as a
surprise to many leaders today, but a great many vendor-partners follow such practices exactly.

They do it every day, but so much cynicism exists
today that they get little credit for doing the right
thing. Basically, too many leaders are incredulous
about human sincerity and goodness and legitimate
kindness and so on. That is something created by society, a sense of paranoia and suspicion.

The reality is that business leaders want partners
who will be there for them through good times and
bad times, and they understand that those partners
have to make profits as well. In fact, the leader wants
his vendor-partners to make profits, wants them to
thrive and survive.

If vendor-partners are unable to make a profit, they
will not be able to provide the continuity desired—the
kind of meaningful discussions that we want. Hon-
estly, how could anyone sit in front of a vendor-partner and "negotiate" a price that will result in that
company's going out of business? What a waste of
time and effort.

It does happen.

Take Vlasic Pickle, which filed for bankruptcy in
2001 because it was unable to be profitable despite
record sales. Negotiated pricing with large, price-

driven companies eliminated its profit margin, though it arguably had the best-tasting pickle in America. Vlasic is now back in business.

The best examples of partnership stem from consulting relationships, not contractual relationships. The best relationships are those that require consultation. The person consulting has expertise that is needed in a certain area, and we sit down and discuss how to make the most effective use of the dollars. That is when we all gain traction, and that is when we form true partnerships.

Partnership is among the most misused words in business today. Tactically, the definition assumes that both parties share the risk and profits together, but we submit that a more strategic definition applies. True partners benefit from working directly with each other. In other words, both companies improve as a result of the relationship.

Please note that nothing precludes working toward tough compromises as long as this means reaching a fair decision. True partners do not care about how tough they are on each other, but they do care about how fair, reasonable, and equitable they are.

Be as tough as you want, but be fair. Being fair has to do with humanity. It has to do with integrity, and it has to do with relationships. These universal truths serve as our apologias for writing this book.

The same principles that apply to dealing with vendor-partners also apply to dealing with customer-partners. But the word *customers* carries a negative connotation these days. In fact, a large telecommunications company announced in 2007 that it was firing thousands of customers simply because they were too "demanding."

At United Supermarkets, we refer to customers as "guests" because the word conjures up an appealing emotional response. It moves us mentally from a position of employee to a position of host or hostess. In turn, we move physically from trying to sell to people to trying to serve people.

No one understands the importance of customer-partners more than Jack Mitchell, author of the book *Hug Your Customers*. Mitchell's business philosophy is rooted in one simple belief: a relationship exists behind every transaction. Rather than surrender to the popular sentiment that over-the-top service is no longer profitable, Mitchell successfully connects with customers using the personal touch. Consider a few practical tips taken from Mitchell's people-first practices:

- A firm handshake
- Sharing the latest joke
- Remembering the name of your customer's pet
- Sharing a cup of coffee
- Opening your business early or late

- A handwritten note
- Knowing your customer's golf handicap
- Letting your customer use your office to make a phone call

Acknowledging your customers as partners casts an entirely different light on business conduct. While it may be lost on many ill-equipped leaders today, the power of nice is every bit as effective in business as it is in church. In fact, it is expected in church, but not in the cold-hearted, cruel world of business.

For many years now, researchers have devoted their energies to determining how companies can compete in a value-driven world. Of the many theories presented, one report delivered by the Rand Corporation caught our attention because of its customer-partner input. In essence, the report revealed five common elements that are vital to customer-partners in every transaction. In no particular order, the data suggested that service, experience, quality, convenience, and price were central to customer-partner buying decisions.

But there was more.

Researchers predicted that for a company to thrive in the value-driven marketplace, it must dominate in at least one element and differentiate in two of the remaining four. Organizations, the report concluded, should seek parity in the remaining two elements. We embraced this idea at United Supermarkets by making it clear inside our organization that we wanted to dominate in the area of service.

Next, we chose to seek differentiation in both the in-store experience and the quality of our products. This meant striving for parity in the areas of convenience and price. As a relatively small regional supermarket chain, we relied heavily on this strategy to mitigate the effects of a high growth in supercenters.

Regardless of which strategy you choose to employ, recognizing customers as partners allows organizations to connect their brands with their customers' emotions. Great brands always make an emotional connection with people. As Starbucks founder Howard Schultz wrote in his book, *Pour Your Heart Into It*, "The most powerful and enduring brands are built from the heart. They are real and sustainable. Their foundations are stronger because they are built with the strength of the human spirit, not an ad campaign."

Schultz has it right, and he backed up his beliefs recently by resuming control of Starbucks, making changes in his management team, and closing every location for three hours during normal operating times to train the 8,000 baristas on how to make a great espresso.

The strength of the human spirit is what drives the relationship between organizations and their customer-partners. This understanding resides in the heart and soul of every properly equipped leader.

However, that is not enough. The leader must become a champion for customers as real people. Leaders must grant permission and empower employees to treat customers with the human spirit.

Our best advice: irrespective of what is popular these days, partners are deserving of humane and ethical treatment, too.

PUNCH LIST

❈ True partners benefit from working directly with each other. Both companies improve as a result of the relationship.

❈ The great majority of so-called advances in business these days, including enhanced profitability, come at the expense of partnerships.

❈ Properly equipped leaders build loyalty to their company among suppliers through the way they treat their vendors.

❈ Organizations that embrace the current system of procurement could find themselves unwittingly tolling the death knell of meaningful partnerships.

❈ Partners support each other during good times and bad times.

❈ Vendor-partners understand the need for lower pricing and can offer recommendations on ways to realize reduced costs. Allowing them a chance to be part of the dialogue pays dividends.

❈ Acknowledging your customers as partners casts an entirely different light on business conduct.

"*It is a paradoxical but profoundly true and important principle of life that the most likely way to reach a goal is to be aiming not at that goal itself but at some more ambitious goal beyond it.*"

—ARNOLD J. TOYNBEE (1889–1975)

CHAPTER  7

PERFORMANCE
(YES, PROFIT)

Properly equipped leaders *want* to serve people, but they also *must* perform for stakeholders.

In other words, a great many leaders today accept the ideas expressed in *Equipped to Lead* and its precursor, *Built to Serve*, but they find it hard to commit to people-first practices and still deliver superior performance. This is a fair assessment. Serving people requires time, money, and commitment.

But this is where conventional teaching and activist thinking part company. Conventional teaching presents the time and money required to serve people as a company expense, a sort of genuflection toward the sanctity of the P&L statement. But activist thinking presents the same information as a company investment.

Sustainability is the result of this equation:

People + Process + Partners + Performance = Sustainability

Failure to properly address any of these components ultimately results in performance failure. Think of it this way: the 4Ps Management System is a scorecard in which people, process, and partners each weigh equally. Performance will be equal to the amount of balance an organization has in these areas.

For example, if we devote only 10 percent of our time and money to people, we will realize a corresponding negative impact on performance. For a simple validation, examine *Fortune* magazine's annual listing of Great Places to Work. You will discover that the companies listed consistently outperform the S&P 500. Why?

We are convinced that it is because those who populate *Fortune*'s list know how to drive the bottom line with people-first practices. They see the time and money they spend on employees as an investment that creates a positive return, not an expense.

The purpose of the 4Ps is to bring order and balance to an organization. This system will allow an organization to replace its current profit-driven business model with a people-first business model leading to profitability. Contrary to what some critics of our work might say, we are happy capitalists. We like profit, but we do not worship profit as our god.

In the 4Ps, performance is more an indicator of health than an indicator of purpose. In fact, not-for-profit organizations can benefit from implementing the 4Ps in the same way as for-profit companies. Please hear this: there is nothing wrong with superior performance, although what constitutes superior performance will vary between not-for-profit and for-profit entities.

We are strong advocates for establishing goals and controls—vital benchmarks for holding the organization accountable. These benchmarks will vary by company and by department, but everyone working inside an organization must always have compatible answers to these five questions:

1. How does my work each day support the vision of the company?
2. How does my work each day support the mission of the company?
3. What is my direct supervisor's name?
4. Do I have the specific tools and training I need to deliver superior performance?
5. How will I know when I have succeeded and the company has succeeded?

Sadly, we repeatedly find that employees in most organizations cannot answer these questions with confidence. It is no wonder that businesses struggle to meet their goals when employees find themselves isolated from the organization's purpose.

Properly equipped leaders can make a huge difference here. Leaders must communicate constantly with employees; it requires a good understanding between leaders and followers.

Too often, ill-equipped leaders think that because the word *communicate* is a verb, it requires action only on their part. For example, they assume that because they sent an e-mail, they communicated successfully. Nothing could be further from the truth. Communication is a serious business requiring a tremendous amount of energy and two-way traffic.

Great communicators deliver something special to employees: access. They connect with people on a personal level. They focus on the hearts of people, not the heartlessness of numbers.

One key aspect of communication is helping people inside an organization prioritize their time and the company's money. Business moves at such a fast pace these days that it is easy to understand why employees are mired in frustration, with too many projects and too little time. Leaders can introduce order and balance to the process of prioritizing with a simple tool that has been used successfully for years.

The prioritization table shown here provides a simple exercise that quickly identifies the most important projects, initiatives, or tasks at hand.

To use the table, we simply list the items we want to make a priority. We can have as many or as few items on a list as we like. Next, we move to Column

A and begin by making a decision between the two priorities by circling the priority (1 or 2) that is most vital at the time. Then we decide between priorities 1 and 3, 1 and 4, 1 and 5, and so on until we reach the bottom of Column A.

Afterward, we move to Column B and begin by deciding between priorities 2 and 3, 2 and 4, and so on. We continue with each column until we are finished. Finally, we count how many of each numeral we have circled. Typically, there will be two or three priorities that are obviously more important than the others.

At that point, we can either run the table again on those key priorities or move directly to a plan of action. The exercise is short and exceedingly effective.

129

PRIORITIZATION TABLE EXERCISE

A	B	C	D	E	F	G	H	I
1 2	—	—	—	—	—	—	—	—
1 3	2 3	—	—	—	—	—	—	—
1 4	2 4	3 4	—	—	—	—	—	—
1 5	2 5	3 5	4 5	—	—	—	—	—
1 6	2 6	3 6	4 6	5 6	—	—	—	—
1 7	2 7	3 7	4 7	5 7	6 7	—	—	—
1 8	2 8	3 8	4 8	5 8	6 8	7 8	—	—
1 9	2 9	3 9	4 9	5 9	6 9	7 9	8 9	—
1 10	2 10	3 10	4 10	5 10	6 10	7 10	8 10	9 10

Designed by Michael Michalko, Thinkertoys

This simple exercise can help employees focus on the most vital needs of any organization. It moves people from a mental state of paralysis to an actionable plan of attack and does it, depending on the number of priorities, within about 15 minutes. Leaders know how to help their people identify action priorities.

Like coaches, business leaders constantly look for the little things that will move people one step closer to fulfilling their potential. That is why we have come to appreciate the 4Ps.

The 4Ps promotes return on investment in humanity (ROIH). The business world promotes cash flow. Period.

Despite the occasional bizarre preoccupation with EBITDA and its misapplication to businesses as a cash-flow indicator, most savvy investors will tell you that cash is king. Why? Cash flow is the best measure of an organization's true profitability.

Frankly, some investors look at EBITDA because it is easy to calculate and it sanitizes the effects of financing large capital investments. Most investors are trained in financial performance, not in people, process, or partners. They limit their frame of reference.

And EBITDA does have its merits. Looking at it as a percentage of sales can reveal whether a company operates efficiently, and it is an effective metric for tracking industry trends and core operating profitability.

But since EBITDA excludes changes in working capital and is not a true measure of cash flow, it is possible for a company to post an enviable EBITDA while losing money because it cannot sell its products. The dot-com fiasco of 2000 was a painful reminder of what can happen when investors fail to acknowledge the importance of negative cash flow.

Many investors also suffer from severe myopia. Performance indicators today measure current results, last year's results, or the last quarter's results. While those metrics have value, they fall short of a more compelling question that investors rarely ask: what was the company's performance relative to its potential for the same period?

This is a relevant and important question. But it is a question that is not asked often enough because any meaningful answer requires true leader engagement in unleashing the imagination and creativity of employees. If leaders are not investing in people, then it is much easier to simply keep comparing performance to historical benchmarks, not future potential.

Investing in people is the most expedient way to improve performance for organizations that are committed to long-term success. While the notion that people use only about 10 percent of their brain is more myth than fact, a verity of modern science is that the amount of information people can absorb is unlimited.

131

This alone ought to convince leaders that they can improve any organization's performance exponentially just by engaging people in a significant way, but it does not.

Too many companies, urged on by anxious investors, resort to cost cutting for quick results. Gordon Bethune, the astute former CEO of Continental Airlines, had it right when he reminded Wall Street analysts that you cannot grow a company by cutting costs. The leaders of a company must address the top line of the P&L at some point.

Sure, cost containment is here to stay, and all organizations need to be prudent in spending their money. But leaders (or investors) cannot back their way into prosperity and still meet all of the stakeholders' needs.

Investors and turnaround specialists sometimes buy and sell companies to make a quick dollar. But while they may profit from the transaction, other stakeholders, namely front-line employees and partners, rarely benefit from the disruptions involved in being bought and sold over and over.

Several years ago, United Supermarkets purchased several stores that had been owned and operated by an independent businessman. We were the fifth owners of these stores in less than a decade. Imagine the reaction of the employees upon hearing that the company had been sold . . . again. At the first orientation meeting with the newest owners, one employee asked, "What kind of uniform this week?"

It took United Supermarkets 11 years to convince those employees that we were committed to their welfare. Once they became convinced, the small group of stores began improving its performance. Eventually, those same stores, staffed largely with the same people, went from a distant third in the marketplace to first.

They have remained at the top every year since. Like Bethune's Continental employees who took the airline from worst to first, United Supermarkets employees did the same thing, but only after our company made consistent investments in the people and recognized their efforts to turn things around.

A small amount of recognition goes a long way toward improving performance. A lot of recognition goes even further than we can imagine. At United Supermarkets, we hold an annual leadership meeting to recognize exceptional performers throughout the organization. Each year, we make an effort to look at performance on a case-by-case basis. We factor in the relative nature of business.

For example, one person we spotlighted was our bakery director. Now, bakery represents less than 2 percent of our company's total volume, but that department, with her leadership, increased its performance and contribution to overhead by 300 percent. As we talked about this great achievement, one person casually remarked, "Yeah, but look at the dollars. It's not that big of a deal."

One of our senior leaders was quick to offer the individual another view, which we embrace: "If you're working every day in the bakery, it is 100 percent of your world, so it's an incredibly big deal." Never allow the size of a contribution to the whole serve as a metric for celebrating achievement. Quite often, even a small contribution in dollars makes a big difference to the organization in other ways.

Such is the case in United Supermarkets' bakeries and floral shops. While the total dollars generated by sales in these departments is relatively small, the impact they have on the overall shopping experience is unquestionably higher than that of most other departments in the store. If we did not consider the impact that the bakery and floral departments have on the entire experience, odds are that those employees would rarely be recognized for anything.

Every employee is deserving of attention—and not merely once a year. Every employee should receive regular, meaningful, personalized feedback. Shockingly, many employees never receive a substantive, candid work assessment. Gallup Poll data suggest that about 35 percent of respondents claim that their supervisor spoke to them only about their weaknesses.

134

Another 25 percent said that their supervisor talked to them about their strengths. Sadly, 40 percent of those polled said that their supervisor did not speak to them about either. Why? Well, for starters, most people see giving feedback as confrontational. Harvard Business School professor James Heskett humorously ranked performance reviews alongside "root canal dental work" on the list of things that managers and employees look forward to each year.

Regardless of how painful they might appear, performance reviews are essential to the long-term success of employees and organizations. Unfortunately, performance reviews have become a topic of great complexity these days. For those companies that are actually tracking and requiring annual reviews, their objectives range from weeding out poor performers to recognizing superstars—and just about everything in between.

For leaders who are intent on fostering a people-centered culture, the annual formal performance review ought to be used as an opportunity to develop talent. We recommend that 80 percent of the time spent in formal performance reviews be devoted to talking about the future.

Unfortunately, performance reviews rarely provide insight leading to meaningful employee development. Shown in Figure 7.1 is an actual performance review that reflects the missed opportunities to provide an employee with practical feedback.

FIGURE 7.1

Performance Review

Productivity - B (Good) : *Your productivity could be better.*

By contrast, Figure 7.2 reveals a more meaningful review—one that an employee can use to improve performance.

Properly equipped leaders conduct routine audits of all reviewers in an effort to ensure that the process is consistent, productive, and fair across the organization.

If leaders are using a system of goals and controls, vital benchmarks that are systematically communicated to and negotiated with employees, as we recommended earlier in this chapter and will detail later in this book, then a leader need not spend more than 20 percent of the meeting recapping successful goal accomplishment. At the same time, we believe in regular, ongoing, and informal feedback to ensure proper skill development.

To maximize employees' potential and realize superior performance, a company must enable its employees to hit their stride. Individual performance is

FIGURE 7.2

Performance Review

Productivity - B (Good) : *Productivity exceeds standards; however, this area could be rated an A (Great) by increasing daily productivity from 8% last year to 10% this year. Consider creating cross-functional work teams capable of expediting projects when things get slow in a team's area. Additionally, review workflow processes to determine if technology enhancements (like digitizing content to create near real time access to files) is appropriate and feasible.*

---

largely overlooked by business today because illequipped leaders rarely take the time to truly understand the potential that their employees have and what kind of impact they can make on other team members as mentors.

At adplex, a young man joined our organization several years ago in an administrative capacity. However, when he went on sales calls, his excitement was almost contagious. We could see the wheels spinning as he flourished in that aspect of the job. He had a real passion for sales that an ill-equipped leader might have ignored, but not in this case.

Instead, he became a key contributor to the company because of a small investment of time on the part of several leaders in the organization. His improvement in performance directly resulted from mentoring.

Recently, the authors asked a panel made up of seven financial professionals to assess the ideas expressed in this chapter. What follows is an overview of their thoughts:

> Companies have to understand people are an investment with tangible costs, including salaries, signing bonuses and training costs. The company then invests in the cost of "ramping up" the new hire in terms of teaching them the culture, mission, vision and values.
>
> The majority of those costs can be calculated, but what about the other side of the equation? What value can be placed on each employee's potential, the training and time invested in that employee and the financial impact that person creates for the organization?
>
> This is a fairly exact science in the world of professional sports, where athletes are paid millions of dollars each season for performing a specialized skill. We wish to go beyond that model, measure the intrinsic value of each person, and carry it to the asset line.
>
> Part of this value can be assessed during the review process, which traditionally looks only at past performance. Reviews should include intangible qualities such

as trust, goodwill, awareness, service and engagement. These intangible factors drive the tangibles just as people drive profits.

Performance reviews ultimately could be fashioned to address each employee's value. If a company were sold, a certain value would be placed on the ability of that company to produce or sell a product. If a company is being purchased, employees are part of that package.

Ultimately, it is a two-way street. The more a company invests in its employees in terms of training and teaching, the more valuable each one becomes. Likewise, the larger the number of well-trained, well-taught employees within a company, the more valuable that company becomes.

It is time spent by the company on the employee and by the employee on the company. It is talent contributed to the company by the employee and it is treasure provided from the company to the employee. Perhaps those components, cornerstones of the faith community, can be blended together into a formula for assessing that most important part of any organization—the human factor.

Remember, it is an equation: Sustainability is a reflection of the investment we make in time and money directed toward people, processes, partners, and performance. That is why ROIH easily supersedes

ROI. Superior performance is more of a journey than a destination. We should always consider and seek what is missing. Where can we improve? How can we effectively adjust?

We realize sustained performance by investing in people, processes, and partners.

PUNCH LIST

❋ Sustainability is the result of this equation:
   People + Process + Partners + Performance =
   Sustainability.

❋ In the 4Ps Management System, performance is
   more an indicator of health than an indicator of
   purpose.

❋ Properly equipped leaders understand that communication involves helping people inside their organization prioritize employees' time and the company's money.

❋ Many investors suffer from severe myopia.
   Performance indicators today measure current
   results, last year's results, or the last quarter's
   results. All of these are important metrics, but they
   fall short of equating performance with potential.

❋ Even a small amount of recognition goes a long
   way toward improving performance.

❋ For leaders who are intent on fostering a people-
   centered culture, the annual formal performance
   review ought to be used as an opportunity to
   develop talent.

"Civilization is a movement and not a condition, a voyage and not a harbor."

—Arnold J. Toynbee (1889–1975)

CHAPTER  8

CALL TO ACTION!

In the fall of 1975, *One Flew Over the Cuckoo's Nest* debuted in movie theaters across the United States. The film, starring Jack Nicholson as a reluctant mental patient, quickly captured the attention of moviegoers and went on to garner five Oscars.

One particular scene in the film resonated with people and, indeed, continues to inspire change across the globe. For example, Russian television journalist and author Vladimir Pozner claims that the scene brought him to tears and redirected his entire life's work.

The scene features Nicholson's character, R. P. McMurphy, trying to escape from a mental institution by picking up a heavy sink and throwing it through an upstairs window. When the sink proves too heavy to lift, McMurphy's fellow patients delight when he falls short of his goal. In the face of debasing criticism, McMurphy turns to his fellow patients and says, "But I tried, didn't I?" The line, delivered with the emotion that only Nicholson could muster, is an inflection point in a compelling story.

In many ways, leaders today are trapped in an asylum of faulty logic and irrational ideas. Like McMurphy, we long for an escape, but it certainly requires both heavy lifting and significant trying. Yes, there will be uninformed critics—mean-spirited people who are content to watch from a distance and disparage our efforts at bringing about change, but do not take it personally.

Their criticism is not so much of you as it is of change—any kind of change. President Woodrow Wilson was right when he said, "If you want to make enemies, try to change something." It is so true. But we must try. And, even in the face of disappointment, we should all be able to make this claim: "But I tried, didn't I?"

Achieving success requires the proper tools. If McMurphy had had the right gear, lifting the sink would have been possible. And, most certainly, others who hoped to flee would have seized the moment to benefit from his accomplishment. This is the nature of leadership: a few people pave the way for a populace, even knowing that that populace includes people who prefer to tear you down rather than build you up.

Take solace in the fact that you are not alone. History is replete with examples of the ever-present "vocal minority"— those uninformed or misinformed detractors who view life in a context of despair rather than a vision of hope. In short, this is the norm—and always will be. Anticipate them and then press on toward what you believe in your heart to be right.

The balance of this book is about moving forward with the necessary tools for success—and escape.

Interestingly, the first tool requires us to review the present before we assess the future. In Chapters 4 through 7, we outlined the 4P Management System and the importance of its simplicity amid chaos. What is needed first is an understanding of how an organization's culture values people, process, partners, and performance.

Keep in mind that organizations may comprise multiple cultures—for example, virtually all organizations have one culture among senior leaders and a different culture among rank-and-file employees.

For this reason, we recommend that all stakeholders participate in providing initial feedback as seen from their point of view. We accomplish this requirement by offering a short list of questions that is easily accessed via the Web at www.equippedtolead.com. Once participants log on to the site, they should provide a special code, found printed on the inside cover of this book's dust jacket.

Survey data provide a leading indicator, not a lagging indicator as many leaders believe. Relevant feedback serves as a wellspring of opportunity, as long as the information is treated appropriately. For example, participants must understand that the survey collects no personal data. Additionally, accurate feedback demands that there be no possible form of retribution. Nothing will sabotage a survey faster than a reprisal against an employee who is seeking to provide honest, albeit unfavorable, feedback.

The 4P Management Assessment contains 10 questions each regarding people, process, partners, and performance. The survey takes less than 10 minutes, and respondents receive immediate feedback regarding their input. Senior leaders may receive customized results by using Go Think! to contact the authors. Contact information appears at the back of this book.

Using a proprietary means of scoring, the answers to the 4P Management Assessment are used to plot graphically the health of an organization as it relates to the necessary balance, helping leaders to maximize their organization's potential. A sample plot in Figure 8.1 illustrates the four quadrants of the 4P Management System. Note that in the sample graph, plotting the employees' perceptions uses a dashed line, while plotting the management team's perceptions uses a dotted line. Both plots are compared to the ideal circumstance—equal balance among each of the 4Ps. The solid line represents the average between employee perception and management perception.

Within each quadrant, five subquadrants appear in different shades of gray. The chart scores the subquadrants using the descriptors Great, Good, Average, Focus, and Repair. It provides numbers to assist in

FIGURE 8.1

4P™Assessment Chart

- - - - -	Employees
....	Management
————	Average

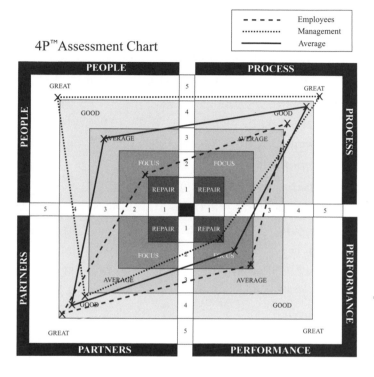

analyzing the magnitude of the respective plots quickly. For example, a score of Great (5 × 5) suggests that the attention being paid to that particular element of the 4P Management System is superb—no additional changes may be necessary.

On the other hand, a plot landing in the Repair (1 × 1) subquadrant suggests insufficient attention, requiring immediate action. Scoring the graph allows leaders to visualize each of the four elements in context with one another.

Simply put, the 4P Assessment Chart serves three purposes. First, if the assessment is taken by an individual, the chart results will provide the individual with his or her assessment of the organization's 4P balance (or imbalance). Second, when employees and management take the assessment as a team, the chart results will provide aggregated feedback on management and employee perceptions and whether they are aligned.

It is common to experience differences of perception between these two groups with regard to one element of the 4Ps. Sometimes dramatic shifts occur, especially in organizations that are trying to merge cultures or digest sweeping change. Such empirical data are invaluable when it comes to understanding and pinpointing areas of disconnect between leaders and followers.

The chart's third purpose is to visually depict areas of imbalance. In the example provided, a clear imbalance exists in the area of performance (a common plot pattern these days). A leader of our sample organization would make the following assessment in a matter of minutes:

1. The *people* quadrant requires immediate action. Despite the perception of management that things are great with people, the employees perceive performance as being more important to the organization than their needs. A major disconnect exists in this quadrant, requiring focus.

2. The *process* quadrant appears exceptionally healthy, and no significant difference exists between employees' perception and management's perception. This requires no additional action.
3. The *partners* quadrant appears healthy, and no significant difference exists between employees' perception and management's perception; no additional action is required.
4. The *performance* quadrant requires immediate action. According to the scoring, the employees recognize the need for additional focus to improve performance; however, management's perception is that *performance* requires repair. A significant misalignment exists between employee perception and management perception.

149

Given that the process and partners quadrants appear healthy, the management team in our hypothetical organization should seek to engage its people in a meaningful way to understand their needs. Once management takes action to ensure that the employees feel valued, a dialogue can occur regarding properly aligning performance goals.

The sample 4P Assessment Chart reflects a common predicament for organizations that are run first and foremost on the basis of financial or accounting benchmarks. Ironically, our research shows that organizations with similar plots ferment frustrations by what appears to be a productivity issue in the eyes of senior leaders.

In truth, the issue has less to do with productivity (process) and more to do with people and their sense of being devalued by the organization. In our sample company, the odds are good that all stakeholders could realize complete satisfaction if employees and management align their perceptions of each other.

This is the irony of organizational excellence: the solutions required to maximize the potential of any organization already exist within the business; however, tools are needed to achieve success.

In the same way that we feel better spiritually the more we give of ourselves to others, performance-driven organizations enjoy greater success the more they connect freely with their employees. After establishing a meaningful line of communication, the real "heavy lifting" follows—identifying issues representing obstacles to success.

When we listen to understand and not to respond, as Dr. Stephen Covey advocates, what typically follows is a long list of concerns or issues residing in the minds and hearts of employees. Our experience has taught us that the most effective way to distill such notes is to apply the prioritization tool outlined in the previous chapter.

Administering this tool allows for two important steps. First, it ensures that by repeating the specific concern or issue, we fully understand what the employees are communicating. Second, it allows us to quickly discover the root causes that are initially creating the list of concerns and issues. Typically, one root cause drives several concerns or issues.

Rarely have we implemented the prioritization tool without discovering something new about ourselves, our people, or our organizations. For example, a group of 12 very energetic associate pastors met at the Go Think! conference center at Go Away Farm for a leadership retreat in 2007. Although the pastors were on the same team, they did not work together daily; however, it became clear that they shared similar concerns and issues.

During the meeting, which was intended to be a planning retreat for the next year, each pastor expressed personal frustrations regarding a wide range of topics that moved the meeting in a different direction from that originally planned. As the pastors spoke out regarding their feelings and perceptions, we compiled a list of each specific concern or issue. By the end of the first session, the list numbered 40 different perceived obstacles.

Upon completion of the prioritization exercise, three root causes became painfully evident to the group. Topping the list was the realization that the modern demands of church economics were robbing them of their calling: sharing the story of salvation with young people. Instead, building the numbers of church camp participants and developing camp activities consumed their focus.

In short, these young associate pastors faced the prospect of being relabeled event planners. As a result, frustration and a lack of fulfillment ensued. What they needed was a return to their calling, which meant a realigned definition of success. No longer was success measured solely on the basis of attendance. Instead, leading young people to Christ again became their primary focus, and as a result, the group became galvanized in its support of one another.

The result was precisely what one might hope: the group members embarked on a journey of establishing specific goals for their organization that were directly tied to their vision or calling. The participants left energized and focused on a specific list of goals and associated action steps necessary to restore both their personal and their professional fulfillment. What began as a planning retreat evolved into a life-changing event—a personal transformation.

Employees and senior leaders in for-profit organizations can benefit in precisely the same manner as the associate pastors of a nonprofit organization, as in the example provided. Many experts offer recommendations regarding the keys to goal setting, but our discoveries reveal that nothing rivals the accuracy of a system that is best remembered by its simple acronym: SMARTA. It was shared with us by our colleague Michael Starr.

Goals must be Specific, Measurable, Action-Oriented, Realistic, Time-Bound, and Aligned with the overall vision and mission of the organization. Our experience teaches us that most organizations struggle with meaningful goal setting. Quite often, what ill-equipped leaders regard as goals are really nothing more than long lists of action steps.

If participants sincerely follow the SMARTA standard, goals lists are short, concise, and vital to the success of the organization. But goal setting is not easy and requires practice and diligence.

For example, one marketing senior executive once reported a goal of publishing four issues of the company magazine annually. His entry prompted a simple question: Why? Why bother to publish any company magazines?

His response was a good one: "I want to improve the communication with our employees." In reality, his response made for a noble goal, but his plan to publish four issues of the company magazine was merely an action step—a numerically accountable means to an end.

153

In order to help the executive discover his real objective, we advocated using employee surveys, which were already being used to derive feedback from employees throughout the company, to establish a success benchmark. Previously, employees had indicated a score of 75 percent regarding whether management did a satisfactory job of communicating with them.

The marketing executive's new goal read: "Improve the communication with our employees from 75 percent to 85 percent as measured by the employee surveys conducted quarterly." The new goal met the SMARTA standards and ensured a higher level of accountability for both the executive and the organization.

Without an existing employee survey, we recommend establishing the following goal: "Develop and implement an employee survey to measure the effectiveness of corporate communications." This goal must allow for a baseline against which you can measure progress.

Similarly, we met with a chief operating officer (COO) once who proudly reported the following goal: "Build more stores." When asked why he wanted to build more stores, the COO replied, "We need to improve our return on assets." After some lengthy discussions, the COO revised his goal to read, "Improve return on assets from 4 percent to 6 percent." Building more stores became an action step necessary to realize the goal.

Take a minute and test your own skill at identifying goals versus action steps. Below are 10 entries taken from goal sheets submitted by senior leaders of organizations. How many of them strike you as legitimate goals for a top-level executive?

1. Visit every store in the chain within the calendar year.
2. Reduce turnover within the first 90 days of employment from 87 percent to 50 percent chainwide.

3. Develop and implement a customer satisfaction index to use as a benchmark for improving customer service.

4. Increase sales from $786 million last year to $950 million next year.

5. Write a policy letter outlining the company's new profit-sharing plan.

6. Make our company a Great Place to Work.

7. Send two executives to Harvard Business School's Advanced Management Program.

8. Reduce store operating expenses from 21 percent last year to 19.5 percent this year.

9. Hold a leadership meeting for all mid-level managers.

10. Administer a no-notice operational assessment for store directors.

155

If you selected entries 2, 3, 4, and 8, then you understand the importance of SMARTA and proper goal setting. Entries 1, 5, 6, 7, 9, and 10 fail to adequately explain their overarching purpose—a key standard for good goal setting. They all may represent worthy action steps, but they fail to reflect the true objective behind the entry.

Admittedly, as goal setting is implemented inside an organization, the specificity changes the closer the process moves toward front-line employees. In other words, front-line employees' goals may reflect more specific action steps, and that is reasonable as long as the action steps support and are aligned with the over-arching goals that senior leaders establish.

The 4P Goals Sheet shown in Figure 8.2 represents what organizations ought to consider using to track goals and action steps. By including the corporate overarching goals for each element of the 4Ps, employees can easily see how their individual goals support the company.

Most organizations that fully embrace goal setting rely on both annual goals and monthly goals to ensure that consistent progress is being made toward successful accomplishment of the organization's vision and mission. Additionally, completed goal sheets become invaluable resources during annual appraisals, as they represent a comprehensive record of employee achievement during the course of the year.

In summary, we have introduced here three foundational tools that are necessary to answer the call to action. First, the 4P Assessment Tool should be administered and the results analyzed within the organization. Second, employees should be engaged to determine any concerns or issues (perceived or otherwise), using the prioritization tool to distill root causes. Third, goals should be established throughout the organization using the SMARTA standard.

While all three tools provide different benefits, they each promote order and balance inside organizations. Individually, the tools we recommend in this chapter have proved effective at assisting leaders in their efforts

FIGURE 8.2

Organization Name Here

Goal and Progress Report _____

Employee: _____

For Period: **From** _____ **to** _____

Corporate Goals	Employee Goals	Tasks Related to Goal	Completed by:
People			
1)	1)		
2)	2)		
3)	3)		
Process			
1)	1)		
2)	2)		
3)	3)		
Partners			
1)	1)		
2)	2)		
3)	3)		
Performance			
1)	1)		
2)	2)		
3)	3)		

157

to maximize performance. When used together, however, the tools represent a systematic approach to stimulating change and ensuring accountability amid the chaos that change can produce inside an organization.

The use of any new tool to aid in an organization's management is not always accepted readily. Sadly, critics look for reasons to impair or even disrupt progress. Unfortunately, every organization, and particularly every large organization, employs impostors—either incompetent employees or those who are disconnected from the organization's vision and mission.

In some cases, organizations may employ incompetent, disconnected people. In any case, masterful impostors locate bureaucratic hiding places. The implementation of goals reveals these hiding places for what they are—hideouts for nonperformers.

A word of warning: impostors will be among the first to resist filling out goals sheets. Why? The light of accountability will illuminate and eliminate their hiding places. All the charm in the world will not redirect the bright light of accountability. This can be a painful process, but it is a process that leaders must embrace if they hope to realize the potential of an organization.

The potential for improved results in every element of the 4Ps warrants implementation. At best, leaders will realize extraordinary success from beginning the process of holding their organizations accountable. At worst, leaders will gain a better understanding of what makes their organization tick and eliminate some impostors along the way.

PUNCH LIST

※ The nature of leadership is that a few people pave the way for a populace, even knowing that that populace includes those who prefer to tear you down rather than build you up.

※ Relevant feedback serves as a wellspring of opportunity, as long as the information is treated in the right manner.

※ In the same way that we feel better spiritually the more we give of ourselves to others, performance-driven organizations enjoy greater success the more they connect freely with their employees.

※ Goals must be Specific, Measurable, Action-Oriented, Realistic, Time-bound, and Aligned with the overall vision and mission of the organization.

※ Most organizations that fully embrace goal setting rely on both annual goals and monthly goals to ensure that consistent progress is being made toward successful accomplishment of the organization's vision and mission.

159

"The right moment for starting on your next job is not tomorrow or next week; it is instanter, or in the American idiom, 'right now.'"

—ARNOLD J. TOYNBEE (1889–1975)

CHAPTER 9

MEASUREMENTS THAT MATTER

Have you ever watched children play a game of T-ball? It is much like baseball, except that the players hit a ball placed on top of a batting tee rather than hitting a ball thrown by a pitcher. Typically, T-ball players range in age from three to seven, and it is common to have both boys and girls on a team.

Having coached and observed quite a few of these games during the past 25 years, one thing remains the same: kids even as young as three want to know whether they won the game.

In the beginning, it seemed appropriate to simply say, "We all won. We all had a good time, didn't we?" But these days, that approach is seen as unacceptable. The reality is that children learn early that the sole objective in life is to win—even if it means beating the pants off a three-year-old who tends to hit the ball and run to third base instead of first.

Measurements start early in life and never really cease. Even in death, someone will most likely write an obituary or prepare a eulogy that attempts to measure the person's accomplishments in life. There is simply no escaping the fact that almost everything gets measured nowadays.

We have no bone to pick with this reality. In fact, we are fundamentally opposed to efforts to eliminate measurements or competition. It is a mistake not to acknowledge individual accomplishments, because doing so perpetuates a deception about life itself—the misguided notion that everyone performs at about the same level. This is a falsehood.

Hard work and perseverance allow some people to outperform others. We find nothing fundamentally wrong with this truth. And it is troubling to see some schools across the country dispense with selecting class leaders such as valedictorians or salutatorians.

However, the real issue today is not in accepting the need for measurements but in developing meaningful measurements. Many measurements used today simply do not hit the mark—they are useless pieces of data that, at best, tell us little about true performance. At worst, they actually mislead us into believing something that is simply untrue.

The increase in corporate writedowns on the heels of subpar quarters, hidden inventory adjustments that inflate operational earnings, and the creation of sister companies or special-purpose entities for concealing the parent company's actual financial condition lead us to question the veracity of organizational measurements these days.

Most of the measurements that are commonly recognized today still provide no real assurance of accountability. While it is true that the Sarbanes-Oxley Act of 2002 radically altered the way for-profit organizations conduct business and gave CEOs something to ponder before attesting to the accuracy of their organization's numbers, the ethical landscape remains less than ideal.

According to the Ethics Resource Center's (ERC) National Business Ethics Survey conducted in 2007, 42 percent of employees observing unethical conduct inside their organizations opted not to report it. In an article written by James Hyatt for CRO Corporation, he quotes ERC President Patricia Harned as saying, "Despite new regulation and significant efforts to reduce misconduct and increase reporting when it does occur, the ethics risk landscape in American business is as treacherous as it was before implementation of the Sarbanes-Oxley Act of 2002."

In part, the flickering embers of unimaginable deceit on the part of executives who misrepresented the truth to their stakeholders are anything but extinguished. The oxygen that is still feeding the fire comes from the constant hot air from stakeholders, who are more diverse today than ever before.

Today's financial stakeholders (comprising investors from around the globe) remain eager to quantify results in the form of ratios identifying profitability, capital adequacy, and liquidity. However, employees are in another camp, asking thought-provoking questions regarding compensation, benefits, career opportunities, and other perquisites because they are eager to compare themselves to their peers.

And, likewise, customers or guests occupy yet another camp; their measurements are framed to determine loyalty or lack thereof. All of these people are knocking on the CEO's front door.

Figure 9.1 provides a snapshot of the variety of stakeholders that organizations must satisfy. Note the corresponding list of measurements that are typically provided to stakeholders seeking to assess the organization's success or failure.

The determination regarding which measurements matter depends largely on each stakeholder's particular interest. If an outside investor were to sink $25 million into our $100 million organization, we would most likely provide any measurement that investor asked for, right? The point is that what matters to one group of stakeholders may mean little or nothing to another group.

We have had many conversations over the years with bankers who are eager to plunge head over heels into financial ratios without so much as one question regarding workforce morale. By contrast, we have seen unions devote hours and hours of haggling with management over compensation and benefits, with precious little regard for the looming bankruptcy of the parent company.

FIGURE 9.1

The 4Ps Category	Traditional Category	What to Measure
People	Employees	Career Path / Tenure Dissatisfaction Goals Potential Referrals Satisfaction / Morale
Process	Operations	Costs IT Uptime, Downtime, etc. Marketing Success (share of customer + share of market) Product Quality Productivity Program Success Service Quality Waste
Partners	Customers & Vendors	Damage & Losses % Decline in Customer Count Dissatisfaction Growth in Customer Count On-Time Delivery % Satisfaction
Performance	Finance	Cash Earnings Ratios Results against potential ROI, ROCD, ROA, etc.

How does a leader remain focused on what matters to the organization while continuing to meet the needs of these diverse stakeholders? This question highlights an important distinction for all leaders who are seeking balance amid chaos. It is critical to understand that stakeholders work *on* the organization while senior leaders work *in* the organization, in the same way that doctors work *on* the patient and antibiotics work *in* the patient. While both are necessary, it is the medicine that ultimately cures the patient, not the doctor's diagnosis.

For this reason, stakeholders are invaluable in examining the various aspects of an organization's health, but it is the leaders who ultimately hold the power to change—the power to heal—organizations. As a result, the measurements employed by leaders working *in* the organization will most definitely differ from those measurements transmitted to stakeholders at the conclusion of another quarter or trimester.

The measurements that matter most to leaders ought not to be those reported at the end of the quarter or trimester, although this is typically the case. Rather, leaders need to operate at a deeper level—a level unseen by stakeholders. To use our medical analogy once again, leaders need to employ measurements that determine the health of the organization at the cellular level.

For example, as we have discussed in previous chapters, it is not uncommon for merchants to publish a weekly newspaper ad. For years, merchants have relied heavily on "beating" the competition in their trade areas by breaking an ad with a low price on a popular item. We have never met a merchant who was interested in the lengthy timeline required to actually assemble the advertisement and prepare it for publication or insertion into the newspaper.

Historically, the process could require a final decision regarding the specific product selected and the corresponding price of the product as much as two weeks before the ad is released to the public. Understandably, stakeholders operating at this level of the company would not necessarily care or appreciate the effort required to build the advertisement.

The measurement that matters most to them is whether the advertisement captured the market's attention and drove traffic to the store. However, a leader working *in* the organization could favorably affect this process by measuring the workflow from the inception of an advertisement to the completion of the job.

Figures 9.2 and 9.3 represent a hypothetical measurement of the advertising workflow process from the origin of a job through its completion. By dissecting the process and measuring the flow of work from start to finish, a leader who is familiar with the organization can collapse the time to market exponentially. Note the changes to the workflow shown in the two figures.

167

In this example, the leader is operating at a level that is unseen by the stakeholders looking for sales at the store. Frankly, the measurement that matters most to that audience has nothing to do with mapping workflows or the system of inputs and outputs—that is not even on the radar screen, nor would we expect it to be. On the other hand, such measurements are precisely what ought to be the focus of equipped leaders.

After all, it is this level of detail that drives the success of larger systems within an organization, in much the same way that the cells of a human being drive the larger systems of a human body—the digestive, circulatory, and respiratory systems.

FIGURE 9.2

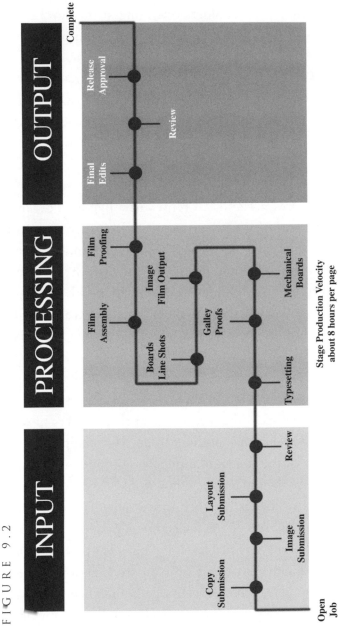

INPUT

Copy Submission

Image Submission

Layout Submission

Review

Open Job

PROCESSING

Typesetting

Galley Proofs

Boards Line Shots

Mechanical Boards

Film Assembly

Image Film Output

Film Proofing

Stage Production Velocity about 8 hours per page

OUTPUT

Final Edits

Review

Release Approval

Complete

168

FIGURE 9.3

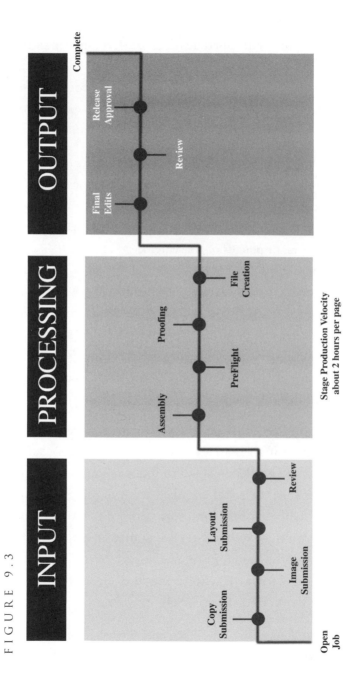

INPUT   PROCESSING   OUTPUT

Open
Job

Copy
Submission   Image
Submission   Layout
Submission   Review

Assembly   PreFlight   Proofing   File
Creation

Final
Edits   Review   Release
Approval   Complete

Stage Production Velocity
about 2 hours per page

169

The best-equipped leaders understand that they ought to be measuring both inputs and outputs at a detailed level. Max De Pree, leadership expert and former CEO of Herman Miller Furniture, explained it this way in his book *Leading without Power*:

> The Soviet Union believed that in many cases managers should be rewarded with bonuses based on input. If you were running a shoe factory, your bonus as a manager was based on how much leather, how many nails, how many pounds of glue entered the process. If all the shoes came out for left feet, well, that was too bad. Nobody cared—except, of course, the people who needed shoes. If you made furniture, your bonus was calculated on how many board feet of lumber entered the plant, not on how many chairs came out. A strange system. We should be surprised not that it disintegrated but that it lasted so long.

Too often, ill-equipped senior leaders become preoccupied with managing the measurements used by their stakeholders instead of focusing on the measurements that their stakeholders want managed.

Nowhere is this conundrum more obvious than in the growth of publicly traded companies such as Starbucks. In his book, *Pour Your Heart Into It*, Starbucks founder Howard Schultz made it clear that people were the key to success. Schultz wrote:

> Our competitive advantage over the big coffee brands turned out to be our people. Supermarket sales are non-

verbal and impersonal, with no personal interaction. But in a Starbucks store, you encounter real people who are informed and excited about coffee, and enthusiastic about the brand.

Once the brand had captured the attention of eager investors, a new group of stakeholders formed—stakeholders who were consumed with building new stores, the measure of their greatest interest. Certainly size has its competitive advantages. Larger companies can spread their administrative expenses over more stores, which improves profitability, and they typically enjoy better buying power and perhaps a larger piece of geographic market share. But side effects will inevitably emerge.

Reflecting on this dilemma (one that is shared by all growth companies), Schultz remarked, "If our competitive advantage has always been the relationship of trust we have with our partners, how can we maintain that as we grow from a company of 25,000 people to one of 50,000?"

This is a fair question because the out-and-out commoditization of the brand hangs in the balance. Stakeholders who believe that the only measurement that matters is growth will most likely never recognize the damage that this growth inflicts on the cellular makeup of the organization's appeal to start with.

It is the leader's responsibility, not the stakeholders', to ensure that the organization remains healthy from the inside out. Hence, a leader's success is determined by substantive measurements affecting the cellular level of the organization. Understanding this distinction between stakeholders' measurements and leaders' measurements allows for sustained success.

Dr. Leonard Berry, author of *Discovering the Soul of Service*, answered Schultz's question—and, in effect, the question of every leader of a high-growth company—when he wrote: "The answer lies in a blend of values-driven leadership, innovative structure, customer- and employee-focused information technology, and ownership attitudes."

This might be a good time for the obvious question, "How many of us are measuring our effectiveness in achieving 'values-driven leadership, innovative structure, customer- and employee-focused information technology, and ownership attitudes?'" These are not common measurements among organizations. Indeed, they are rarely, if ever, addressed in an annual report. Nevertheless, they remain critical to scaling an organization and sustaining success along the way.

So, what keeps leaders from developing measurements that truly matter? First of all, it requires hard work. We prefer to paint with a broad brush as leaders—in fact, for many leaders, the very idea of painting with a fine-point brush is nauseating. It demands more time and requires more attention to detail.

Second, it is in direct conflict with much of what we have read or been taught regarding leadership and the need to be a generalist and not get bogged down in the detail.

Such teachings appear innocuous on the surface, but leaders who want to become better equipped take these teachings out of context more often than not. Leaders must be willing to be in touch with their followers if they are to fully understand their organization and its challenges. Sometimes, leaders devote more time to sending out memos from their office than they do to developing actual meaningful relationships with front-line employees.

Legendary basketball coach John Wooden understood the importance of detail and organization in leadership. In the book *The Essential Wooden*, coauthored with Steve Jamison, Wooden wrote these compelling words regarding practices at UCLA:

> The three-by-five cards I carried kept the train running on a tight, fast schedule. They contained the entire day's practice broken down minute by minute—what we would do from 3:30 to 3:35 and from 3:35 to 3:45, at which time I'd blow my whistle to stop and call out the next sequence, which might be a three-on-one conditioner for seven minutes followed by a different five-minute drill. Each and every aspect of the process—including precisely what everybody was supposed to be doing as well as when and where it would be done—was painstakingly etched on each card. . . . Everything had a purpose; everything was done efficiently and quickly. The whole thing was synchronized; each hour offered up to 60 minutes, and I squeezed every second out of every minute.

Organization was the measurement that mattered most to Wooden. In fact, he said, "Without it I wonder if the UCLA basketball team would have won a single national championship under my supervision. Unlikely perhaps. Organization was one of our superstars." Basketball fans, and aspiring leaders of organizations, will recall that winning, the popular measurement that matters most in sports, was normal for Wooden.

His place in history is secure: 10 men's basketball national championships in 12 years; 7 consecutive national championships; an 88-game winning streak; a 38-game winning streak in NCAA Tournament play; 12 Final Four appearances in 14 years; and 4 perfect seasons. Not bad for a coach who never mentioned winning or a scoreboard as a worthy measurement.

Business, like basketball, is a grind—not in the sense that it is routine, dull, or tedious, but in the sense that it requires constant study and consistently hard work. Having bought, built, and nurtured organizations for nearly three decades, we remain convinced of one thing: rarely, if ever, is there such a thing as easy money (legally).

Despite what may be the hopes and dreams of entrepreneurs around the globe, our experiences reveal that one must be prepared to work hard and, more important, that it should be the journey that delivers the greatest satisfaction—even more than the destination.

Perhaps by now you are connecting the dots as they relate to equipping leaders for greater accountability and success. Know this: the quality of *your* effort is the measurement that matters most. Stakeholders, like sports fans, will always have their own measurements that matter to them. However, we are not fans cheering (or booing) a team; we must be leaders inspiring teams to realize their potential. Our accountability to ourselves is foremost.

When we focus on discovery inside our organizations—the road less traveled, taking us deep within the soul of the business—we find that there is much we can do to appreciably alter the popular benchmarks used by stakeholders who do not have the same perspective as the leader. This requires understanding the details and, more important, understanding the measurements necessary to achieve sustained success.

In looking back over decades of firsthand experience and centuries of documented examples, we have arrived at the same conclusion as Vernon Parrington in sizing up Benjamin Franklin as a leader in the book *Main Currents in American Thought*.

> There was in America a society which valued the things Franklin did well: work hard, write effectively, plan improvements, conciliate differences, and conduct public affairs with popular needs and interests in view.

America still values these qualities, although some specific stakeholders may not. Properly equipped leaders operate using these principles because they are universal, timeless truths that are capable of withstanding any attack.

Finally, we would certainly be remiss if we did not remind readers of this axiom: what gets measured gets done. Though it might sound like a bit of a cliché, the accuracy of this claim is astounding. We look at the claim through a different lens from that used by most people. Typically, business-minded pundits point to the need for bonuses and other compensation to track specific measurements. This is a fair approach to ensure that rewards are tied to results.

However, another reason for understanding and embracing the axiom can be found, one that has less to do with rewards and more to do with mapping. The measurements that leaders embrace most send clear signals regarding the road map for the entire organization. In other words, if we claim to have a goal of becoming a Great Place to Work company listed in *Fortune* magazine, then we must measure our progress in those areas that our employees consider important to our becoming a great place to work.

By the same token, if we claim to have a balanced approach to business, embracing the 4Ps equally, but the only measurements that seem to matter to the leaders are financial, we are making a disingenuous claim. Stakeholders are trusting in that they expect leaders to do what they say they are going to do.

No stakeholder wants to be hoodwinked.

And leaders do not want to be robbed of their integrity, at least not leaders who are in their right minds.

PUNCH LIST

❈ The real issue today is not in accepting the need for measurements but in developing meaningful measurements.

❈ Today's financial stakeholders (comprising investors from around the globe) remain eager to quantify results in the form of ratios identifying profitability, capital adequacy, and liquidity.

❈ Leaders understand that stakeholders work *on* the organization while senior leaders work *in* the organization.

❈ The best-equipped leaders understand that they ought to be measuring both inputs and outputs at a detailed level.

❈ Too often, ill-equipped senior leaders become preoccupied with managing the measurements used by their stakeholders instead of focusing on the measurements that their stakeholders want managed.

❈ It is the leader's responsibility, not the stakeholders', to ensure that the organization remains healthy from the inside out.

❈ Business is a grind—not in the sense that it is routine, dull, or tedious, but in the sense that it requires constant study and consistently hard work.

"Civilizations die from suicide, not by murder."

—ARNOLD J. TOYNBEE (1889–1975)

CHAPTER 10

SUCCESS AND WELLNESS

"How do you define success?"

When we are speaking to groups across the country, this subject often arises. Is success the achievement of something planned or attempted? Or, is it the attainment of fame, wealth, or power? These are important questions because the answers will largely drive our behaviors. In addition, understanding the definition of true success allows us to recognize the biggest threat to achievement today—and it may surprise you.

Without question, determining what constitutes success is a topic that has been on people's minds for centuries. Back in the early 1900s, the *Lincoln Sentinel* solicited essays of 100 words or fewer best defining success. The winner received $250 as well as publication of the essay in the newspaper. The winning essay, entitled *Success*, written by Bessie Stanley, remains quoted frequently today:

> He has achieved success who has lived well, laughed often, and loved much; who has enjoyed the trust of pure women, the respect of intelligent men and the love of little children; who has filled his niche and accomplished his task; who has left the world better than he found it whether by an improved poppy, a perfect poem, or a rescued soul; who has never lacked appreciation of Earth's beauty or failed to express it; who has always looked for the best in others and given them the best he had; whose life was an inspiration; whose memory a benediction.

180

Works by other essayists or poets, including Harry Emerson Fosdick, Elbert Hubbard, and William Henry Channing, among others, also capture the essence of what Stanley suggested in her 1905 masterpiece.

However, something has changed. During the past century, it seems, the more common definitions of success have come to have less to do with the enduring, intangible nature of satisfying the soul and more to do with the ephemeral, tangible nature of satisfying the stomach. People seem less interested in a definition of success that reflects selflessness and more interested in a definition that reflects narcissism.

Lee Iacocca, the colorful American industrialist best known for his leadership in resurrecting Chrysler in the

1980s, faced this question from a young college student following a speech on social values: "How did you become such a success?" Iacocca responded by asking his own question of the audience: "What makes you people think I'm a success?"

Iacocca had his own ideas regarding success; in particular, he rejected the conventional thinking that success should be determined by wealth. That was his style, and it still is to this day. In his book *I Gotta Tell You*, written with Matthew Wayne Seeger, Iacocca recounts one of his more memorable and influential speeches, in which he offered his observation of society's perspective on success. He said,

> We're really upside down. In a completely rational society, teachers would be at the very tip of the pyramid, just above "king," not near the bottom. In that society, the best of us would aspire to be teachers, and the rest of us would have to settle for something less. Passing civilization along from one generation to the next ought to be the highest responsibility and the highest honor anyone could have.

181

We could fill volumes with different definitions of success, but, frankly, we believe that a few observations are necessary to equip leaders properly. First, success, regardless of its definition, should never be considered a zero-sum game. In other words, one person's success does not always require another person's failure. And, second, the biggest obstacle to a leader's success has less to do with dealing with the chaos found in business and more to do with dealing with the stress that such chaos causes.

We will attempt to address both observations in some detail. First, on the subject of defining success using winners and losers, the popularly held notion is nothing more than a myth perpetuated by ignorance. Let us be clear: competition involves winners and losers, but success is an entirely different matter. If success meant winning every game, every sales pitch, every mission, then we would be discounting the efforts of at least half of all participants.

This kind of thinking is dangerous and, equally important, personally and organizationally destructive. When we step back and apply this logic to current events, the fallacy of such thinking quickly becomes apparent. For example, the United States PGA Tour conducts nearly 50 sanctioned events each year. Roughly 150 players will play the tour in either an unconditional or a conditional status.

If we apply the logic that success is defined by winning, then at the conclusion of the season, at least 66 percent of all contestants should consider themselves losers. If the 150th-ranked golfer, playing in a conditional status, could somehow break into the top 100 and secure unconditional playing status for the next year, would that be considered success? Of course.

Tiger Woods, arguably the greatest golfer ever to play the game, has repeatedly made his own thoughts known regarding the fluctuations that we human beings (and organizations) experience. In Dr. Gio Valiante's book *Fearless Golf*, Tiger is quoted:

> While I am warming up before a round of golf I am just trying to understand my parameters that day so if I need to, I can take away 20 percent of my game, cut the golf course in half, and limit my errors. It isn't me at my best, but a lot of times it takes bogey out of the equation, and lets me survive until I can work it out on the range afterward.

Think about what Woods is saying. The number one player in the world defines success often as simply surviving until he can work things out while practicing later. On any given day or in any given year, our definition of success may require review—and that is perfectly acceptable. We can apply Woods's logic to organizations and their leaders.

Success cannot be defined merely on the basis of profit or loss. As in the PGA Tour example, success will most likely be defined differently depending on the organization, its business objectives, and its talent. At the highest level, success should always reflect sustained achievement. And what does "achievement" represent in this context? It represents the realization of a person's or an organization's potential at some particular time.

Returning to the sage advice of UCLA coaching legend John Wooden, "Over and over I have taught those under my supervision that we are all given a certain potential unique to each one of us. Our first responsibility is to make the utmost effort to bring forth that potential in service to our team. For me, that is success. . . . Success may result in winning, but winning may not result in success."

We have provided these snapshots—Stanley's award-winning essay, Iacocca's memorable comments, Tiger Woods's philosophy, and John Wooden's view of success—to arrive at this conclusion. Leaders need to understand this five-point organizational leadership creed:

1. I will seek a proper perspective on my pursuits relative to life itself.
2. I will commit to teaching and coaching at the highest level.
3. I will devote time to my own continuing education.
4. I will accept my organization's unique parameters.
5. I will maximize the unique talents that my organization possesses.

Properly equipped leaders recognize the value of this creed and embrace it because its elements are both timeless and essential to success and sustained achievement.

The acceptance of such a creed allows leaders to moor themselves so that the storms of organizational life cannot tear their teams apart. In the absence of such principles, the stress of dealing with chaos day after day will take its toll on leaders, jeopardizing sustained achievement.

That brings us to our second observation: stress is one of a leader's greatest obstacles to success. Leaders must recognize that wellness is an equally important part of being equipped to lead.

The emphasis on wellness inside organizations is just beginning to create widespread interest among stakeholders. In 2007, for example, the Center for Corporate Culture advanced the idea that sustained organizational success was a function of building upon four foundational pillars: Leadership, Culture, Execution, and Wellness. The center's first official conference attracted nearly 200 CEOs from around the country who were eager to develop specific initiatives supporting each pillar.

Dr. Kenneth Cooper, founder of the Cooper Clinic in Dallas, Texas, and the physician who first coined the word *aerobics* in the late 1960s, delivered the keynote address. "Everyone should desire to live a long and active life followed by an exceedingly short death," Dr. Cooper told the audience, setting the stage for his persuasive presentation.

At the center of Dr. Cooper's philosophy is the idea that we should adopt a paradoxical mindset regarding wellness. In other words, in much the same way that our spiritual journey requires acceptance of the idea that the more we give of ourselves in service, the more meaning and fulfillment we find in our lives—a paradoxical concept—so it is with such things as stress.

For example, Dr. Cooper often hears questions like, "Can stress heal?" Using data obtained through the Cooper Institute, one of eight divisions of the Cooper Clinic, Dr. Cooper shared the following personal ideas regarding wellness and stress:

1. *The emotional paradox:* Accept and acknowledge stress as a fact of life, and the changed attitude alone may be enough to cause the stress to disappear.
2. *The fitness paradox:* Gently pushing yourself physically, even to the point of temporary discomfort, can create a positive turnaround that lasts.
3. *The creativity paradox:* Creativity is enhanced when an overloaded mind is no

longer pushed. Learn the principle of releasing and retreating. Many times a step back is a move forward.

4. *The success paradox:* Release your ambitions. Goals can be achieved more effectively and readily by letting go and refusing to push so hard.

5. *The productivity paradox:* Working less sometimes can produce better results than driving oneself.

6. *The relationship paradox:* The best relationships may be characterized by controlled conflicts. Couples who have been together for decades might have wonderful marriages, but they will not agree on everything. These differences in opinion make life interesting.

7. *The spiritual paradox:* In a mysterious way, true spiritual serenity and inner strength emerge just when life seems most unsettled.

Notwithstanding nearly five decades of Dr. Cooper's constant refrain regarding the value of wellness, only recently has our society begun to relate wellness to sustained achievement.

More important, empirical data suggest a striking correlation between behavior and health issues among employees, especially in the area of stress and productivity. The evidence is virtually impossible to deny and garners more attention these days because of skyrocketing health-care costs. For example, the *Wall Street Journal* reported in April 2005 that obese General Motors employees were costing the company nearly $1.4 billion in health-care costs each year.

In fact, health-care costs have more than doubled, from 7.2 percent of GDP in 1970 to 16.2 percent in 2005. The figure is expected to swell to 22 percent by 2015. Studies show that 50 to 70 percent of total health-care costs are behavior-driven. What is needed today is a health-care system that is designed to drive healthy behavior—beginning with prevention and wellness.

188

In the summer of 2006, the Center for Creative Leadership initiated a research project to determine how stress affects leaders. The compelling report, released in 2007, revealed this partial listing of relevant findings:

1. Of the leaders surveyed, 88 percent say that work is a primary source of stress in their lives, and having a leadership role increases the level of stress.

2. More than 60 percent of the leaders surveyed cite their organizations as failing to provide them with the tools necessary to manage stress.

3. More than two-thirds of the leaders surveyed believe that their stress level is higher today than it was five years ago.

4. Nearly 80 percent of the leaders surveyed say that they would benefit from a coach to help them manage stress.

5. A lack of resources and lack of time are the most stressful leadership demands experienced. Stress is caused by trying to do more with less and trying to do it faster.

As you can see, leaders have much to do to improve their health and that of their people, which, naturally and most definitely, improves the health of their organizations. Judging from the data, a good place to begin is learning how to deal with stress using the paradoxical approach that Dr. Cooper advocates and embracing wellness as a foundational pillar.

How do you handle stress in your life? Do you have a way of gauging the stress level you are experiencing for a given stage of life? The editors of webmd.com offer a quick survey to determine your particular stress level. The questions are easy to answer and reflect everyday issues.

For example, the survey asks if you feel tired or have a lack of energy, if you have trouble sitting still or concentrating, and if you have problems getting to or staying asleep at night. Online resources such as www.webmd.com routinely offer surveys related to stress and provide immediate feedback. Understanding your stress level is important to building a meaningful wellness program that is best suited to your needs. All organizations, regardless of industry, ought to be paying attention to the well-being of their people and their consumers.

The food industry, for example, is more focused on wellness today than at any other time in its history (regrettably, the bar was embarrassingly low). Good things are happening, and some companies are beginning to make measurable progress.

In terms of consumer wellness, Indra Nooyi, the gifted chairman and CEO of PepsiCo, is steering the company toward making a profound difference. In the 1990s, 100 percent of the company's U.S. portfolio was "Fun for You" treat products. Today, nearly 45 percent is "Good for You" or "Better for You," and the company is well on its way to achieving 50 percent or more by 2010.

How does PepsiCo's new strategy result in success? Nooyi defines true success as "performance with a purpose." In Nooyi's case and that of PepsiCo's, the purpose is clearly representative of a *higher* principle.

In terms of organizational wellness, Steve Burd, Safeway's chairman and CEO, is spearheading a campaign within his company and realizing positive results. Central to Safeway's success is a strong preventive-care program, with 100 percent coverage of annual physicals, well baby/child care, and other age-appropriate procedures, such as breast and prostate cancer exams, colonoscopies, and other important screenings.

The program was unveiled in 2006, and 44 percent of the nonunion workforce enrolled. By the end of 2007, more than 70 percent of eligible employees were taking advantage of incentives and education, demonstrating solutions that can serve as models for improving wellness throughout all organizations.

According to the Coalition to Advance Healthcare Reform (CAHR), Safeway reduced health-care costs by 15 percent in the first two years compared to an average increase of 10 percent in the previous year. As a result, participating employees experienced a 25 percent to 34 percent reduction in their annual total health-care costs. But we can glean something that is of even greater importance.

In speaking with Burd about the success of the program, he quickly points out that the wellness initiatives he started have created a greater sense of trust and loyalty between senior leaders and front-line employees. Even union leaders are taking notice and beginning to lend their support. Not only are organizations beginning to acknowledge the importance of wellness, but a few are determined to make it a non-differentiator in the marketplace. In other words, these companies are willing to share the results of their wellness initiatives. They view wellness, like food safety, as beneficial to everyone.

Steve Burd walks the talk. He exercises daily, often in the wellness facility constructed on the campus of Safeway's corporate headquarters. For those leaders who are not assigned to the home office, Burd makes every effort to ensure arrangements with local fitness clubs in cities where Safeway employees reside.

Kraft Foods is also leading the way in terms of wellness for its employees. Its corporate vision is to build an organization of healthy, high-performing employees who are fully engaged in their work, taking personal responsibility, and feeling rewarded. To aid in the realization of that vision, Kraft offers employees in the United States 100 percent coverage for annual physicals and health screenings, as well as education, disease management, and assistance to support well-being and identify and manage health risks.

Also, Kraft offers programs and discounts for weight management and fitness. Health-decision support is provided through personal health coaching and online tools and resources. Kraft's Healthy Living Reward Program allows employees to earn up to a $200 annual credit toward medical plan contributions for participation in Healthy Living programs and activities.

Incentives also include quarterly drawings for prizes valued at $2,500. Kraft's many wellness programs work together to manage total health. The employees receive the right support and information at the right time, without disruption or confusion, and without redundant efforts or costs.

In 2007, United Supermarkets developed its own wellness program in conjunction with services offered by the Cooper Clinic. Executives and their spouses are provided with annual physical examinations and nutritional counseling at no charge. The company plans to extend those benefits in the future.

Other companies are following PepsiCo, Safeway, and Kraft in their commitment to wellness, and many have joined the CAHR. As of the release of this man- uscript, more than 50 companies were actively seeking to reform health care and promote wellness within their organizations. For a complete listing of CAHR member companies and their success stories, log on to www.coalition4healthcare.org.

The bottom line regarding wellness and success is straightforward: the more we put into one, the more we get out of the other. Imagine a world in which the definition of true success centered on serving and enriching people's lives. Furthermore, imagine a world in which organizational leaders, in recognition of the definition of true success, committed to the overall wellness of themselves and their employees.

What would the world of "work" look like then?

We can answer that question.

We would discover that the more we give, the more we receive.

Paradoxical?

So be it.

PUNCH LIST

❈ Ineffective leaders seem less interested in a definition of success that reflects selflessness and more interested in a definition that reflects narcissism.

❈ Success, regardless of how anyone defines it, should never be considered a zero-sum game. In other words, one person's success does not always require another person's failure.

❈ Success cannot be defined merely on the basis of profit or loss.

❈ Stress represents a leader's greatest obstacle to success. Leaders must recognize that wellness is an equally important part of being equipped to lead.

❈ Leaders have much to do to improve their health and that of their people, which, naturally and most definitely, improves the health of their organizations.

"The human race's prospects of survival were considerably better when we were defenseless against tigers than they are today when we have become defenseless against ourselves."

—Arnold J. Toynbee (1889–1975)

CHAPTER 11

FAILURE IS NOT AN OPTION

Before we plunge into the reasons why *failure* is not an option, it seems logical that we would define failure—especially given the last chapter's effort to define *success*. In Chapter 2, we referred to the strengths movement fueled by the wisdom of Marcus Buckingham.

While there are some important differences between Buckingham's teachings and those found in this book, the idea that failure is not the opposite of success (excellence) is a certainty upon which we can all agree.

Webster's Dictionary may list *failure* as an antonym for *success*, but properly equipped leaders of organizations do not. In the eyes of senior leaders, true failure has only one definition: giving up.

The odds are good that we all have heard this definition at one time or another, but many sociologists slowly have come to grips with this idea. Candidly, it seems pretty obvious that failure cannot simply mean falling short of something.

Imagine for a moment accepting such a premise. Babe Ruth struck out 1,330 times in his 8,399 at-bats, Abraham Lincoln lost seven elections before winning the presidency, and Albert Einstein's doctoral dissertation was rejected, but we rarely speak of those distinguished people in terms of their failures. Instead, we celebrate their successes in terms of their perseverance.

The same holds true for organizations. Coke sold an average of just nine bottles a day in its first year, but we would be denying the world's number one brand, according to *BusinessWeek*, the recognition it deserves if we suggested that it is rooted in failure.

Macintosh's first computers were "crappy" (Guy Kawasaki's word, not ours) because they lacked software, hard disks, slots, and color, but we would be denying the remarkable innovation that the models represented in the context of the other products of the era if we suggested that they were rooted in failure.

Failure is not the opposite of success. Failure occurs only when we give up—when we stop believing in ourselves or in others. Failure occurs when we surrender all hope. For this reason, failure is not an option.

Hope is found in the understanding that most of the gloom of organizational chaos is directly tied to circumstances that we have the power to change. Properly equipped leaders are genuine in their belief in and acceptance of this maxim.

Joni Eareckson Tada is the founder and chief executive officer of Joni and Friends, an organization dedicated to Christian ministry. Joni is also a quadriplegic. Confined to a wheelchair in 1967 after a diving accident, Joni had every reason to give up on life. But, after two years of rehabilitation, she emerged with new skills and a passion for assisting others with similar disabilities.

Her autobiography, *Joni*, became an international bestseller. A full-length motion picture also chronicled her incredible journey. Today, Joni travels the world, serving and enriching the lives of others. She is the author of more than 35 books and a frequent keynote speaker throughout the world. Despite her disability, she has visited more than 40 countries, ministering to millions of people who are seeking her advice, wisdom, and hope.

Joni's story is the ideal segue to an important lesson regarding the resiliency of the human spirit—particularly when we recognize the source of that spirit: God. Properly equipped leaders recognize the authenticity of every human being. They know that authenticity comes not from material wealth but from God, the Creator.

This dictum leads us to two critical epiphanies. First, human beings are the lifeblood of every organization.

Second, every human being has a purpose in life, whether or not that human being knows or embraces it.

No story coming out of the twentieth century captures the essence of these two epiphanies as well as the account of the legendary Oscar Schindler. Set against the backdrop of World War II and the Nazi death camps in which millions of Jews were murdered, Schindler, once an opportunistic businessman and Nazi collaborator, rose above it all with extraordinary compassion and the highest regard for humanity to save the lives of more than 1,000 Jews.

His story, retold by director Steven Spielberg in the film *Schindler's List*, won seven Academy Awards but, more important, brought millions of people to a greater understanding of the Holocaust.

While the film contains many compelling scenes, none is more moving than the last, which features Schindler, played by Liam Neeson, addressing more than 1,000 workers gathered together during the fall of Nazi Germany.

Recognizing that his business partnership with the Nazis would jeopardize his life after the war, Schindler is hurriedly preparing to flee Germany, but first he must say good-bye to the workers for whom he had expended his fortune and risked his life. Overwhelmed with guilt, Schindler's film character delivers these haunting lines to his Jewish friend Itzhak Stern:

SCHINDLER: I could've got more—I could've got more,
    if I'd just—I could've got more—
STERN: Oscar, there are eleven hundred people who are
    alive because of you. Look at them.
SCHINDLER: If I'd made more money—I threw away so
    much money, you have no idea. If I'd just—
STERN: There will be generations because of what you
    did.
SCHINDLER: I didn't do enough.
STERN: You did so much.
SCHINDLER: This car. Goeth would've bought this car.
    Why did I keep the car? Ten people, right there. Ten
    people, ten more people. *(He tears a Nazi pin from
    his lapel.)* This pin, two people. This is gold. Two
    more people. He would've given me two for it. At
    least one. He would've given me one. One more. One
    more person. A person, Stern. For this. I could've
    gotten one more person and I didn't. I didn't . . .

201

The story of Oscar Schindler reminds us of the
authenticity of every human being. A generation of
Jews survived certain death in Nazi gas chambers
because one man devoted his life and his fortune to
serving and enriching their lives.

In what way does Joni's story inspire you? How
does the account of Oscar Schindler's Jews affect the
leaders of organizations in the twenty-first century? Or
is it anachronistic to suggest that there is a connection?

How do the actions or inactions of today's leaders affect the next generation of workers?

These examples remind us that failure is not an option because nations of human beings deserve better. According to a May 2007 study released by the Economic Mobility Project, an initiative of the Pew Charitable Trusts, the health and status of economic mobility in America may be in serious jeopardy.

The study's coauthors, John E. Morton, managing director of Pew's Economic Policy Initiatives, and Isabel V. Sawhill, senior fellow at the Brookings Institution, highlight America's current predicament in the prefacing comments of the report, entitled *Upward Mobility: Is the American Dream Still Alive?* They write:

> For more than two centuries, economic opportunity and the prospect of upward mobility have formed the bedrock upon which the American story has been anchored—inspiring people in distant lands to seek our shores and sustaining the unwavering optimism of Americans at home. From the hopes of the earliest settlers to the aspirations of today's diverse population, the American Dream unites us in a common quest for individual and national success. But new data suggest that this once solid ground may well be shifting. This raises provocative questions about the continuing ability of all Americans to move up the economic ladder and calls into question whether the American economic meritocracy is still alive and well.

Frankly, we need considerable inspiration to exercise our power to change what is already a difficult circumstance in America. While we are still regarded as the world's greatest superpower, we are now also regarded as the world's largest debtor nation. In a speech delivered to the National Press Club on December 17, 2007, Comptroller General David Walker said:

> Believe it or not, the federal government's total liabilities and unfunded commitments for future benefits payments promised under the current Social Security and Medicare programs are now estimated at $53 trillion, in current dollar terms, up from about $20 trillion in 2000. This translates into a de facto mortgage of about $455,000 for every American household and there's no house to back this mortgage! In other words, our government has made a whole lot of promises that, in the long run, it cannot possibly keep without huge tax increases.

The study goes on to reveal that American men who were in their thirties in 1974 had median incomes of about $40,000, while men of the same age in 2004 had median incomes of about $35,000 (adjusted for inflation). As a group, income for this generation has averaged 12 percent lower than that of their fathers' generation.

"While factors other than cash income also contribute to economic mobility," according to the report, "these data challenge the two-century-old presumption that each successive generation will be better off than the one that came before."

Another survey, conducted by the Pew Research Center in May 2006, indicated that barely a third of adults expect the next generation to grow up to be better off. There is real cause for concern—for most of the American workforce, the gap between earnings and productivity growth is continuing to widen.

Popular television host and best-selling author Lou Dobbs, a Harvard graduate, speaks and writes on this subject with a great sense of passion and urgency in his book *Independents Day*:

> For too long the American people have deluded themselves that failures in leadership will in the fullness of time resolve themselves in our great republic because our history has given us assurance that partisanship is an acceptable substitute for citizenship. We've accepted our own apathy and tolerated what has become a frontal assault by the establishment elites on our national sovereignty, the welfare of our people, and our future as a nation.

Dobbs contends, and rightly so, that our two-party political system is no longer effective because gerrymandering and other oddities about the process have created a system of extremes, which has resulted in gridlock. Given that the nation's founding fathers desired a system that would imbue collaboration and compromise, it is hard to argue that Dobbs is incorrect.

Washington used to be made up largely of moderates who were capable of reaching across the aisle, but it is now largely lacking in meaningful political discourse. John F. Kennedy's astute advice, "Let us not seek the Republican answer or the Democratic answer, but the right answer," seems to have been forgotten in a country of growing partisanship.

This could become a dark chapter in many ways, but an answer does exist. It has little to do with politics or politicians and almost everything to do with businesses and properly equipped business leaders. The stakes are exceedingly high, not just for our generation, but for succeeding generations as well. Failure is not an option—although it would be easy to see why someone might give up when comparing our $12 trillion economy with our $53 trillion in unfunded potential liabilities.

We have the power to change, but we need the courage and discipline to begin immediately. So, how do we begin? What exactly should we do? Here are ten steps that every organizational leader should commit to without delay:

1. Set personal pride aside and acknowledge that we need God's forgiveness, and pray for His divine intervention to restore our principles, human rights, and higher purpose for existence.

2. Place people first in every business decision we make. Seek daily to help front-line employees discover

their life's purpose. Devote every day to serving and enriching the lives of others.

3. Develop a coalition of passionate business leaders to reform the local school system. Be a volunteer to teach civility and leadership. Reduce overcrowding in the classroom through private funding of facilities, create incentives for all teachers to remain current and competent in their field of expertise, and work with the local school board to restore discipline in the classroom.

4. Join the Coalition to Advance Healthcare Reform (CAHR). Effectively dictate policy to legislators by demonstrating that business leaders can improve health care, implement wellness programs, and reduce the overall costs of taking care of people. Lead the way by exercising and being fit.

5. Stop spending beyond our means, both personally and organizationally. Educate directors to reject investors who demand growth and unreasonable profits and who express little, if any, regard for the importance of remaining faithful to the vision and mission of the organization's founder(s).

6. Vote. Encourage others to register and do the same. Run for office, but only if we have the energy to do something and enough money not to be subject to anyone. Hold politicians accountable.

7. Support institutions dedicated to spiritual growth in our area, and encourage every human being to be active in ministry and charitable work. Give

back to the community all that we can—not just what the tax laws allow.

8. Take care of the elderly, beginning with our own families. Devote whatever time is necessary to ensure that their golden years are the best they can be. Assist our children in altering their demanding schedules so that they can spend time with their grandparents and elderly relatives.

9. Support the military and provide employment for service members leaving active duty. Hold jobs for service members who are assigned to the National Guard or Reserves so that they can fulfill their service to our country.

10. Implement the 4P Management System. Never hold another meeting without discussing people, process, partners, and performance—in precisely that order. Make money, but do it ethically.

207

If organizational leaders follow these ten steps, the challenges we face may not all be met right away, but we will affect and arrest many of the trends that are continuing to exacerbate our problems.

In fairness to Lou Dobbs's sense of frustration over what is happening in America, he is also quick to point out there are now "promising signs that the American people will soon be ready to reclaim this nation." It is already happening in many pockets of the country. Properly equipped leaders are stepping up and creating positive changes.

Marsha Sharp is one of those leaders. A successful college women's basketball coach at Texas Tech University for 24 years and a 2003 inductee into the Women's Basketball Hall of Fame, Sharp retired in 2006 to pursue a new vision.

Working tirelessly with Dr. Kitty Harris-Wilkes, director of the Center for Addiction and Recovery at Texas Tech, Sharp launched United Future Leaders, an innovative program to teach values such as civility, ethics, and leadership to fifth- and sixth-grade students.

The program is a model for replication in communities across the country. The vision of influencing an entire generation of youngsters to avoid drug use and other destructive behaviors will most definitely alter and better the future of the communities in which these children live.

Texas businessman Steve Trafton sold his family's printing operation in 1998. He remained at the helm of the company for the next several years, reporting a steady flow of exceptional performance achievements to the parent company.

Eventually, though, Steve and his wife, Rajan, felt called to ministry—helping to heal and restore broken marriages. The couple created the Hideaway Experience at their ranch on the rim of the Palo Duro Canyon near Amarillo, Texas.

Partnering with skilled, licensed counselors devoted to Judeo-Christian principles, the Traftons spend most of their time these days in prayerful meditation and intercession on behalf of couples who have lost hope for their marriages.

Remarkably, the Hideaway Experience has saved 93 percent of the marriages of people who attend, although these couples had all but given up. Like United Future Leaders, the Traftons' ministry is a model for replication in communities across the country.

Similarly, David Miller had a successful career as a businessman and entrepreneur. After selling the Med Group, a national service provider in the medical equipment industry, Miller founded Spirit Ranch, nestled in the Escondido Canyon five miles north of downtown Lubbock, Texas. Miller and his staff facilitate team-building sessions and leadership development training for families as well as people in business, education, government, and religion.

209

Since opening the facility in 2005, Spirit Ranch has hosted thousands of participants who desired spiritual and leadership encouragement. As a result, organizations are being favorably influenced by the experiences and testimonials of the leaders who have attended. Miller's Spirit Ranch is another model for replication in communities across the country.

Sharp, Harris-Wilkes, Trafton, and Miller are merely four examples of leaders with the power to change the world—the power to create a better future. They are not waiting for a government mandate, nor are they standing still waiting for federal funding. They are moving to rescue children, marriages, families, and communities at a time when many Americans have given up on children, marriages, families, and communities.

In short, they are proactively delivering solutions because the stakes are high; failure is not an option.

Properly equipped leaders see the potential, not the unlikelihood. In nations and organizations and families today, we can lay claim to something that God afforded all of us: the power of choice. We have the power to change the world because we have the power to make alternative choices in the future—choices that celebrate the potential of our endeavors and the promise found in unending hope.

Failure is not an option because failure requires us to give up, to quit. What does stand between us and success, however, is a thick wall of malaise created by a misguided culture that is marked by individualism above all else. The only way to breach this wall is to recognize that we have some serious pick-and-shovel work ahead. What we need now is steady progress— each leader doing his or her part with the help of his or her organization, his or her community.

It is possible for properly equipped leaders to change everything and make it better than it was before. We have the power. Let the work begin.

PUNCH LIST

※ The idea that failure is not the opposite of success (excellence) is a certainty upon which we should all agree.

※ Failure occurs only when we give up—when we stop believing in ourselves or in others. Failure occurs when we surrender all hope.

※ Human beings are the lifeblood of every organization, and every human being has a purpose for life, whether or not that human being knows or embraces it.

※ We have the power to change, but we need the courage and discipline to begin immediately.

※ Properly equipped leaders are stepping up, and positive changes are occurring.

※ Properly equipped leaders see the potential, not the unlikelihood.

"History is a vision of God's creation on the move."

—Arnold J. Toynbee (1889–1975)

CHAPTER 12

SUCCESS STORIES—REAL INSPIRATION

We have spent a great deal of time discussing the need for better-equipped leaders to adopt people-first practices, but a number of companies already grasp this concept and are on the cutting edge when it comes to unleashing the incredible potential and power of purposeful people.

In this final chapter, we will provide examples of these companies, many of which have been recognized by the Great Places to Work Institute as examples to which other companies can aspire.

For example, Qualcomm is one of those companies that "get it" when it comes to empowering the workforce. Qualcomm has built its corporate culture on three principles: integrity and trust, open communication, and respect for individuals. The company's work environment is built around employee contributions, with an emphasis on the personal freedom of each individual.

The result: Qualcomm gets high marks from the Great Places to Work Institute when it comes to building credibility between the company's leaders and its workforce. Qualcomm's inclusion among the Top 100 Best Places to Work for the past nine years attests to its effectiveness.

Among its many innovations in this area, Qualcomm created a concept known as QC Daily News, a Web-based news vehicle designed primarily for internal communication. The company made sure that all of its thousands of employees had access to this content, all of which was generated internally and aligned with the corporate values of Innovate, Execute, and Partner.

Qualcomm also produces an annual report about its people. The project recently completed its second year, and the report is released in conjunction with the shareholder report, providing stakeholders with a simultaneous look at fiscal and human accomplishment.

The report about people is produced in both Web and print form. It includes highlights from every division within the company, providing success stories that connect the workforce throughout the organization to the company's vision and mission.

Included in the content are messages from the company CEO and president, stories about employees, a look at accomplishments during the year just completed, partner stories, and stories of inspiration from employees.

Qualcomm also used technology to create an Innovation Network, an online forum where employees can submit ideas, which are compiled and reviewed by senior management members. This creative approach allows employees to share their expertise in a virtual brainstorming atmosphere. Employees receive points for ideas and earn prizes for reaching certain point levels.

Another example is Lincoln Plating, a metal-finishing company based in Lincoln, Nebraska, that earns high marks for its workplace culture, based on this belief: "Knowing who you are tells what the vision can be." Lincoln Plating also believes in selecting employees rather than hiring them, crafting a culture of treating people respectfully as human beings.

Among its many strengths, the company's corporate wellness program is considered among the best in the country. In Lincoln Plating's performance management system, a wellness component is tied to overall performance and pay. The company's wellness package includes incentives for tobacco cessation and weight management, as well as programs, newsletters, and seminars. Employees are reimbursed for fitness club memberships, and family members can participate in the program, called *Go! Platinum*, at no charge. The goal is to reach the Platinum level in fitness, which includes achieving flexibility, body fat, weight, and blood pressure targets.

Lincoln Plating believes that healthy people make more productive employees who bring a positive attitude into the workplace and have a positive impact on the world as citizens. The company also recognizes achievers in the program through Monthly Champion events that culminate in a Night of Champions, celebrating a year of wellness accomplishments throughout the organization.

What is the payoff for this kind of wellness initiative? Company representatives say that annual workers' compensation claims declined from $500,000 to $50,000. In addition, the company's health-care costs are 40 to 50 percent of the U.S. average. Lincoln Plating officials say that their nonunion company has a per-person wellness budget of $224. Wellness has been built into a culture of encouragement and celebration. The successful balance achieved by Lincoln Plating is giving employees permission to have fun while understanding that wellness is a serious issue.

Arnold & Porter, a law firm based in Washington, D.C., has set the bar high when it comes to inclusiveness. The company took a proactive approach to diversifying its workforce and turned to its employees to help make it happen.

First, the firm created employee groups focused on increasing minority and female representation in the workforce. A number of practices emerged from those groups, including expanded recruitment, expanded involvement of currently employed minorities in the hiring process, and a top-down diversity training program. The firm also implemented a policy of promoting work-life balance and backed it with financial incentives.

Second, Arnold & Porter implemented a series of accountability measures. Through the process, the firm learned seven lessons:

1. The best ideas will come from below, but diversity policies must be pushed from the top.
2. Diversity means diverse, and training must include everyone.
3. Without accountability measures, success is impossible.
4. Retention leads to recruitment.
5. One size does not fit all when it comes to approaching diversity.
6. Good diversity practices equal good business practices.
7. Diversity efforts require full-time, focused attention.

Similarly, Recreational Employment Inc. (REI) and its more than 8,000 employees have broken new ground in corporate giving and in its environmentally friendly approach to doing business. The company's corporate giving initiatives began in 1976, and it put a Stewardship Initiative in place in 2002.

With more than $1 billion in annual sales, REI is the largest consumer co-op in the country, and it is among the top ten, as rated by the Environmental Protection Agency, for its renewable energy purchases. Since its founding, the company has grown, but its leaders have insisted on smart growth to preserve its unique culture.

REI's three-pronged emphasis is on Planet, People, and Community, and the company targets strategies directed toward those important entities through active leadership, shared vision, and engaged employees. REI has a deep belief in preserving the planet, and its Stewardship Initiative focuses on five impact areas:

1. Climate change and energy
2. Paper and forest products
3. Waste reduction and recycling
4. Green building
5. Product stewardship

REI accomplishes this through a clearly focused vision that is applied consistently and communicated broadly. It takes a similar approach to community involvement. The focus is on conservation through volunteerism, recreation through the promotion of an active lifestyle, and youth through the creation of advocates within the next generation.

The company aligns its financial resources with its human resources in a powerful way. When employees donate to organizations, REI matches the donation up to $1,000. Company officials said that this practice keeps the finance department busy; some 900 checks are cut each month. The practice results in an engaged workforce. In 2000, REI employees hosted 33 community service projects. A mere six years later, employees hosted 527 projects while accumulating 900,000 hours of service.

The company's Peak Program, aimed at creating environmental awareness in young people between the ages of 6 and 18, has enjoyed a similar swell in popularity: it reached 3,000 children in 2002 and 126,000 in 2006.

REI's successful national programs are all driven by employees and have a measurable impact. The company takes understandable pride in its recent decision to donate $1 million to the National Parks Service, with each of 100 parks to receive $10,000.

Sustainable companies understand that building a people-first culture requires more than a vocal CEO; it takes employees and partners who are willing to embrace and share it. That philosophy is a cornerstone at David Weekley Homes, a company based in Houston, Texas, that has been included among the best places to work a half-dozen times. The company, founded by then-22-year-old David Weekley more than 30 years ago, firmly believes that employees stay or leave a company as a direct result of the influence of their supervisor.

David Weekley Homes believes that an effective culture involves a sense of purpose, something to work for that is more than a paycheck; allows for a deep sense of satisfaction and an understanding that what employees do is good *and* right; and serves a noble cause.

One of the company's core values is this mantra: "If it's almost right, it's wrong." Employees are brought into the culture with a clear grasp of the organization's core values of Integrity; Superior Product; Expect the Best, Bring Out the Best; and Excellence. The company's leaders believe that the purpose of a company should be (does this sound familiar?) to enrich people's lives.

David Weekley Homes pays particular attention to the manner in which new employees enter the culture, believing that providing a firm foundation is the best way to build a sense of purpose and belonging into each and every new hire.

It takes place in three stages of the employees' tenure:

1. Recruiting and hiring: they sell it.
2. Coming on board: they instill it.
3. Growing and developing: they live it.

The approach begins during the hiring process. The company has a rigorous interviewing process that includes time with multiple managers within the organization as well as team and peer interviewing. Potential new hires also complete assessments, and company executives spend time with the "key influencers" in the life of a potential hire, such as a spouse. At David Weekley Homes, the belief is that everyone is a potential customer or team member.

Upon completing the hiring phase, the new employee comes aboard in style. Employees attend Weekley 101, an intensive two-day orientation session that includes a heavy dose of Web-based learning, a visit with David Weekley, a standing ovation from everyone else in the workplace, and an opportunity to build a home (with LEGOs).

The company schedules professional growth reviews regularly and treats feedback as a company-wide gift. The culture includes team meetings and an open environment of communication in which everything is shared. David Weekley Homes regularly recognizes employees for their achievements and accomplishments. Its advice: when you celebrate, celebrate big.

Each of these five companies shared its best practices during a recent Great Places to Work Conference. They represent only a few of many companies that are committed to making the workplace a savored experience, not a dreaded burden.

And they are not alone.

Wegman's, a 90-store retail grocer on the East Coast, has emphasized the importance of helping employees strike a balance between work and life. The company developed a Web-based system known as the

Labor Resource Manager to avoid overburdening employees and ensure that they had support from their colleagues at the busiest times.

The tool also created flexibility in helping employees care for sick family members, pursue degrees, or take a summer off to pursue a passion. The next step is to incorporate a mentorship element into the program.

W. L. Gore, a manufacturing company based in Delaware, has adopted a team-based approach to hiring that is marked by consistency, regardless of position. The company's work culture is unstructured and there are no traditional bosses, creating a need to find people who have initiative and self-motivation. Gore puts more stock in the candidate's potential contribution over the long term than in his or her short-term ability to get a job done.

At the Container Store, with headquarters in Dallas, Texas, a Fun Committee is charged with building intimacy among employees through lunchtime activities such as a silent auction. Once a week, employees gather for a huddle to share time-sensitive information and introduce new employees.

New hires are welcomed with Foundation Week, an orientation to the company, its products, and its philosophy. Stores join hands with their respective communities through private preview parties scheduled for the evening before a store officially opens.

Valero Energy Corporation, headquartered in San Antonio, Texas, has established a Valero Volunteer Council, a self-governing group of employees who provide volunteers for worthy causes. Volunteers have donated as much as 140,000 hours of time to a variety of pursuits, including mentoring students, organizing fund-raisers, participating in community cleanup events, and working at youth centers.

The company's mission statement, "Take a leadership role in communities by providing company support and encouraging employee involvement," is displayed at all locations and given to all new employees as a wallet card. Valero has led the nation in per capita giving, with San Antonio employees contributing more than $1,000 per person; the company once gave $6.5 million in employee and corporate gifts to the United Way.

Valero recognizes and celebrates its spirit of community service in high-profile ways. The company presents a Volunteer of the Year Award each year, with a committee at each location reviewing and selecting a winner from its site. Recipients receive a designer watch and plaque and are honored at a luncheon with their senior leadership team.

At Root Learning, a consulting firm based in Sylvania, Ohio, programs, plans, and initiatives that affect employees are developed through a collaborative decision-making process, effectively blending opinions and viewpoints from management and employees. Even the company's mission and vision statements emerged from a series of meetings in which employees were encouraged to participate.

The system, "Broad-Based Opt-In Dialogue," means that each person and each team has the right and the responsibility to engage in dialogue with others on any topic that is important to their daily work. The company also recently launched a program called RISE, or Root's Internal Stock Exchange, as a part of its annual planning process. This stock exchange of ideas allows employees to suggest ideas for benefits or programs.

The Four Seasons Hotels and Resorts, generally acknowledged as the gold standard for hospitality, has a three-stage management-specific orientation program in which new managers perform the uniformed duties of those under their supervision to gain a full understanding of and respect for each position.

Finally, Men's Wearhouse is another company that has it right. From CEO George Zimmer and his unmistakable voice to the rest of the organization, an understanding is in place that Men's Wearhouse may sell clothes, but in the end, it is all about the employees. According to the company's Web site, it dedicates itself to the following core values: nurturing creativity, growing together, admitting to mistakes, promoting a happy and healthy lifestyle, enhancing a sense of community, and striving to become self-actualized people.

Employees receive extensive training that is designed to emphasize personal and career development, employee empowerment, and building high-quality relationships with colleagues and customers. Employees attend comprehensive initiation programs and a series of continuing education seminars.

Men's Wearhouse is also generous with its financial resources. Employee benefits include stock-option opportunities, sabbatical leaves, tuition reimbursement, and a wellness program that includes financial incentives for smoking cessation.

These companies, and many more too numerous to include here, have it right. The people are the real power of an organization. Putting them first cannot come second. As we have made clear, order and balance are realized when leaders adhere to the 4P Management System. Ill-equipped leaders will continue to struggle against the chaos found in their organizations; however, properly equipped leaders deliver peace and purpose to their work. And, in doing so, they will create a legacy of hope among their followers.

We can only hope that readers of *Equipped to Lead* will align their beliefs with their practices.

AFTERWORD

What makes a leader effective in an organization? In trying to answer that question, the book spoke to me on many levels, because as a financial analyst for many years, I have observed and studied the actions of thousands of executives and hundreds of chief executive officers. During that time, I have come to identify what I believe are six keys to success shown time and time again by these leaders.

It should come as no surprise that my observations tie together with many of the powerful points made by Dan Sanders and Galen Walters in *Equipped to Lead.*

I believe these six factors can be identified as keys to success for leaders navigating the world marketplace today:

1. A genuine enthusiasm, passion, and advocacy for their business, expressed both internally to employees and externally to customers, suppliers, and other constituents
2. A clear vision of where they want to take their company, coupled with commitment to adhering to that view, regardless of the circumstances

3. Knowledge of the details of their business, combined with an understanding of how those details fit into the big picture

4. An ability to inspire and motivate their employees, suppliers, and customers

5. An ability to balance delivering short-term results with making long-term investments and a willingness to fight the populist tide of conventional wisdom

6. And perhaps most important, a consistent willingness to promote the "we" of the organization and not just the "I"

At the same time, I believe there are four clear paths to failure that I see hindering success by executives:

1. A preoccupation with short-term results and quick "fixes"

2. A dazzling communication of a vision that is not accompanied by processes to accomplish that vision in their organizations

3. Too much emphasis on acquiring other companies to grow that vision, without taking the sometimes hard steps necessary to truly combine the organizations

4. A fundamental failure to display high levels of integrity (One's actions always become apparent over time.)

Dan and Galen outline the 4P Management System and provide the following formula: people + process + partners + performance = sustainability. Those four critical components will create balance in an organization and are important in any blueprint for success. Likewise, their terminology challenging leaders to look for a return on their investment in human capital, rather than simply seeking financial results, is a call to arms for many organizations.

I have noticed that outsiders tend to believe that people in an organization are motivated only by financial rewards. My own observations suggest that the best motivation leaders can provide to their employees is to show them that, as part of the company, they are making a difference in the world and that they are part of a true "winning team." People who are proud of what they do tend to work harder in their jobs; it really isn't just about the money.

As an analyst, I can relate to comments in the book about "EBITDA"; I see and use it regularly to determine a company's profitability. Appropriately, the authors make an important distinction between EBITDA, which I would say is an example of a company looking good on its surface, and its operating cash flows, found by digging a little deeper, which they eloquently remind us is a better measure of the real health of a company.

Along those same lines, one of the biggest clues about the health of an organization can be found in employee turnover, particularly in the turnover of those in a position to become future leaders in that organization. Even if the financial results look good, if I hear about employee turnover along these lines, it gives me pause. Dan and Galen remind us of how important it is to constantly and consistently value those whom you oversee.

Likewise, I think those who read this work will appreciate the excellent distinction drawn between a goal and an action plan. I find that too often on Wall Street, the world in which I live, the focus is strictly on numbers. In some cases, those numbers may be provided by a CEO who will highlight a particular growth goal that might actually sound more like an action plan. The authors do a superb job in outlining the differences and the impact each can and does have on an organization.

Finally, *Equipped to Lead* impressed me in one other way. Dan and Galen are experienced CEOs. I was struck by their ability to not only express their views so articulately but also to tie them together with examples from their own real-world experiences. When they tell me how their company took care of a cancer-stricken employee or how they wrote a six-figure check to cover a promise they didn't have to keep, it is more than theory. It is a personification of a leader's life in the real world.

It is one thing to pronounce your beliefs about leadership. It is another to open the window of your soul and allow others an up-close look. Within those two stories lies the power and simple beauty of *Equipped to Lead*.

That view cannot be missed—particularly by those who wish to be properly equipped.

Lawrence C. Marsh
Managing Director, Equity
Research, Lehman Brothers

INDEX

Mitchell, Jack, 119
Moral obligation, 8, 9
Morton, John E., 202

N
Nash, Laura, 106–107
National Transportation
    Safety Board
    (NTSB), 100
Natural laws, 8, 9
Nooyi, Indra, 190
NTSB (National Trans-
    portation Safety
    Board), 100

O
*One Flew Over the
    Cuckoo's Nest* (film),
    143–144
Operational execution, 7
    (*See also* Processes)
Order, 1, 5, 9, 52–53
*Overspent American,
    The* (Juliet Schor),
    20–21

P
Parrington, Vernon, 175
Partners, 105–123

aggregation by,
    109–111
antagonistic
    relationship with,
    106–108
building loyalty in,
    108–109
churning, 116–117
customers as, 119–122
fairness between,
    118–119
in 4Ps Management
    Assessment, 149
in 4Ps Management
    System, 10, 106
handling of errors
    with, 111–114
profits of, 117–118
trust among, 114–115
Passion, 33–49
    channeling, 38–39,
        45–46
    and concept of com-
        mon purpose, 37–38
    contained, 39, 40,
        46–48
    encouraging, 40–45
    and skills of leaders,
        36–37

ABOUT GO THINK!

Nobody has time to think anymore—truly think. Or to analyze, brainstorm, build relationships, discover new things, or turn dreams into realities. Go Think! does only that. We facilitate effective thinking that makes effective action possible. We believe in the value of intellect, curiosity, experience, enthusiasm, and instincts. We thrive on working with brands that evoke passion. Also, we are interested only in the long haul—taking brands from one place to the next, to the next, to the next. You get the idea. We aim for a continuous cycle of imagination, sound thinking, research, big ideas, and loud conversations that drive results.

Our approach is simple. We like to *dig into* your business situation through interviews, site visits, research, and competitive assessments—whatever it takes for us to understand your brand and your challenges. We call it *brand interrogation*: we interrogate until the brand confesses its strengths and reveals opportunities. Next, we help you *go away and think*—literally and figuratively. We have a unique first-class conference facility in a barn on a remote 86-acre farm off the beaten path in central Texas. It is an exclusive, private environment where reflecting and thinking are easy. From this solitude and quiet comes incredible thinking, and ideas flow. You are able to concentrate, regroup, reassess your priorities, and reengage in your life's purpose.

For more information on Go Think!, visit

www.goawayandthink.com

ABOUT THE CENTER FOR CORPORATE CULTURE

The Center for Corporate Culture became reality in 2007. It represented a new business standard while advocating an ongoing conversation about the importance of building a workplace culture that is engineered for maximum performance.

The planting of the seeds for The Center's evolution occurred in 2003, when The Dollins Group produced the first in a series of Ethical Leadership Conferences. These successful conferences have featured world-renowned speakers: Dr. Stephen R. Covey, Ken Blanchard, President George H. W. Bush, and General Norman Schwarzkopf. These brilliant thinkers engaged audiences and helped lay the foundation for The Center, which will continue this tradition of excellence by focusing on leadership, ethics, wellness, and execution.

The Center's mission is to advocate an emerging twenty-first-century business model at a time when business leaders face a bold new marketplace in which competition is fierce, consumers are educated, and innovation is the chief currency. The Center is dedicated to helping CEOs and their teams focus on building a sustainable culture while enhancing their bottom line.

To learn more about The Center for Corporate Culture and the opportunities it offers, visit

www.thecenterforcorporateculture.com

or address correspondence to

18333 Preston Road, Suite 220
Dallas, TX 75252